The

Alistair

methuen | drama

LONDON · NEW YORK · OXFORD · NEW DELHI · SYDNEY

METHUEN DRAMA
Bloomsbury Publishing Plc
50 Bedford Square, London, WC1B 3DP, UK
1385 Broadway, New York, NY 10018, USA
29 Earlsfort Terrace, Dublin 2, Ireland

BLOOMSBURY, METHUEN DRAMA and the Methuen Drama logo are
trademarks of Bloomsbury Publishing Plc

First published in Great Britain 2022

A catalogue record for this book is available from the British Library.

A catalog record for this book is available from the Library of Congress.

ISBN: PB: 978-1-3503-2984-3
ePDF: 978-1-3503-2985-0
eBook: 978-1-3503-2986-7

Series: Modern Plays

Printed and bound in Great Britain

To find out more about our authors and books visit
www.bloomsbury.com and sign up for our newsletters.

THE ROYAL COURT THEATRE PRESENTS

The Glow

By Alistair McDowall

The Glow was first performed at the Royal Court Jerwood Theatre
Downstairs, Sloane Square, on Monday 24 January 2022.

The Glow
By Alistair McDowall

CAST (in alphabetical order)

Fisayo Akinade
Rakie Ayola
Tadhg Murphy
Ria Zmitrowicz

Director **Vicky Featherstone**
Designer **Merle Hensel**
Lighting Designer **Jessica Hung Han Yun**
Composer & Sound Designer **Nick Powell**
Video Designer **Tal Rosner**
Movement Director **Malik Nashad Sharpe**
Associate Costume Designer **Helen Lovett Johnson**
Assistant Director **Rosie Thackeray**
Fight Director **Bret Yount**
Associate Movement Director **Blue Makwana**
Stage Manager **Sunita Hinduja**
Deputy Stage Manager **Sophie Rubenstein**
Assistant Stage Manager **Han Randall**
Dresser **Adam J Rainer**
Sound Operator **Robert Schüssler**
Show Technician **Maddie Collins**
Set built by **Miraculous Engineering**

From the Royal Court, on this production:

Casting Directors **Amy Ball & Arthur Carrington**
Company Manager **Joni Carter**
Production Manager **Simon Evans**
Stage Supervisor **Steve Evans**
Lighting Supervisor **Matt Harding**
Lead Producer **Chris James**
Sound Supervisor **David McSeveney**
Costume Supervisor **Lucy Walshaw**

The Glow has been generously supported with a lead gift from Charles Holloway.

Further support has been received by members of *The Glow* Production Circle. *The Glow* was the 2018 Pinter Commission, an award given annually by Lady Antonia Fraser to support a new commission at the Royal Court Theatre.

The Royal Court Theatre and Stage Management wish to thank the following for their help with this production The Globe Theatre, Sparks Theatrical Hire, The Young Vic Theatre.

The Glow
By Alistair McDowall

Alistair McDowall (Writer)

For the Royal Court: **all of it, X, Talk Show (Open Court).**

Other theatre includes: **Zero for the Young Dudes! (NT Connections); Pomona (Orange Tree/ National/Royal Exchange, Manchester); Brilliant Adventures (Royal Exchange, Manchester/Live, Newcastle); Captain Amazing (Live, Newcastle/ Edinburgh Festival Fringe/UK tour).**

Fisayo Akinade (Cast)

For the Royal Court: **Pigs & Dogs, The Crossings Plays.**

Other theatre includes: **Shipwreck (Almeida); The Antipodes, Antony & Cleopatra, Barber Shop Chronicles (National); The Way of the World, Saint Joan, The Vote (Donmar); The Tempest (Globe); Barbarians (Young Vic); As You Like It (New Wolsey/UK & European tour); Refugee Boy, Waiting for Godot (Leeds Playhouse); The Edge (New Diorama); Neighbours (HighTide).**

Television includes: **Dangerous Liaisons, Heartstopper, Atlanta, Silent Witness, A Very English Scandal, In the Dark, A Midsummer Night's Dream, Ordinary Lies, Cucumber, Banana, Fresh Meat.**

Film includes: **The Personal History of David Copperfield, The Girl with All the Gifts, The Isle.**

Rakie Ayola (Cast)

For the Royal Court: **On Bear Ridge (& National Theatre Wales); Breath, Boom, Ashes & Sand.**

Other theatre includes: **Strange Fruit, The Rest of Your Life (Bush); The Half God of Rainfall, King Hedley II (Kiln); Leave to Remain (Lyric, Hammersmith); Harry Potter and the Cursed Child, The Curious Incident of the Dog in the Night-Time (West End); King Lear (Royal Exchange, Manchester); 4.48 Psychosis, Crave (Crucible, Sheffield); The Winter's Tale (RSC/UK tour); In the Next Room (Theatre Royal, Bath); Welcome to Thebes (National); Twelfth Night (Bristol Old Vic); Dido Queen of Carthage (Globe); Hamlet, Twelfth Night (Birmingham Rep/ UK tour); Up 'N Under, The Merchant of Venice (Sherman, Cardiff).**

Television includes: **Alex Rider, The Pact, Grace, Anthony, Noughts & Crosses, Shetland, No Offence, Vera, Midsomer Murders, Under Milk Wood, Stella, Silent Witness, My Almost Famous Family, Doctor Who: Midnight, Holby City, Sea of Souls, Canterbury Tales, Being April.**

Film includes: **Been So Long, King Lear, Dredd, Now Is Good, Sahara, The I Inside, The Secret Laughter of Women, Great Moments in Aviation aka Shades of Fear.**

As executive producer, film includes: **Twelfth Night.**

Radio includes: **Dr Who: Time War II, Reading from Happiness, Foursome, Three Strong Women, Death & the King's Horseman, The Devil's Music, The Erl King, The Bloody Chamber, Torchwood.**

Awards include: **BAFTA for Best Supporting Actress (Anthony); Black British Theatre Award for Best Female Performance in a Play (On Bear Ridge).**

Rakie is a patron of Childhood Tumour Trust and Eclipse Theatre and is a trustee of Actor's Children Trust.

Vicky Featherstone (Director)

For the Royal Court: **Living Newspaper, Shoe Lady, all of it, On Bear Ridge (& National Theatre Wales) [co-director]; Cyprus Avenue (& Abbey, Dublin/ MAC, Belfast/Public, NYC), The Cane, Gundog, My Mum's a Twat [co-director], Bad Roads, Victory Condition, X, How to Hold Your Breath, God Bless the Child, Maidan: Voices from the Uprising, The Mistress Contract, The Ritual Slaughter of Gorge Mastromas, Untitled Matriarch Play, The President Has Come to See You (Open Court Weekly Rep).**

Other theatre includes: **What If Women Ruled the World? (Manchester International Festival); Our Ladies of Perpetual Succour (& National/ West End/International tour), Cockroach (& Traverse), 365 (& Edinburgh International Festival), Mary Stuart (& Citizens, Glasgow/ Royal Lyceum, Edinburgh), The Wolves in the Walls [co-director] (& Tramway/Lyric, Hammersmith/UK tour/New Victory, NYC), Enquirer [co-director], An Appointment with the Wicker Man, 27, The Wheel, Somersaults, Wall of Death: A Way of Life [co-director], The Miracle Man, Empty, Long Gone Lonesome (National Theatre of Scotland); The Small Things, Pyrenees, On Blindness, The Drowned World, Tiny Dynamite, Crazy Gary's Mobile Disco, Splendour, Riddance, The Cosmonaut's Last Message to the Woman He Once Loved in the Former Soviet Union, Crave (Paines Plough).**

Television includes: **Pritilata (from Snatches: Moments from 100 Years of Women's Lives), Where the Heart Is, Silent Witness.**

Vicky was Artistic Director of Paines Plough 1997-2005 and the inaugural Artistic Director of the National Theatre of Scotland 2005-2012. She is the Artistic Director of the Royal Court.

Merle Hensel (Designer)

For the Royal Court: **ear for eye, a profoundly affectionate, passionate devotion to someone (-noun), X, The Mistress Contract.**

Other theatre includes: **Under Milk Wood, Top Girls, Protest Song (National); Enemy of the People (Guthrie, Minneapolis); Macbeth [costume], The Shawl, Parallel Elektra (Young Vic); Arden of Faversham (RSC); Much Ado About Nothing (Royal Exchange, Manchester); Macbeth (National Theatre of Scotland/Lincoln Center, NYC/Broadway/Japan tour); Green Snake (National Theatre of China); Glasgow Girls (& national tour), 27, The Wheel (National Theatre of Scotland); Shun-Kin (Complicité); The Girls of Slender Means (Stellar Quines Theatre Company); Diener Zweier Herren (Schlosstheater, Vienna); Ippolit (& Schauspielhaus, Zürich/Münchner Kammerspiele), Der Verlorene (Sophiensaele, Berlin); Kupsch (Deutsches Theater, Göttingen).**

Opera includes: **Until the Lions (Opéra National du Rhin); Maria Stuarda (Vereinigte Bühnen, Mönchengladbach/Krefeld); Der Vetter Aus Dingsda (Oper Graz); Lunatics (Kunstfest Weimar); 'Münchhausen, Herr Der Lügen' (Neuköllner Oper, Berlin).**

Dance includes: **The Barbarians In Love [costume], Sun, Political Mother (Hofesh Schechter Company); Contagion (Shobana Jeyasingh Dance); 8 Minutes (Alexander Whitley Dance Company); Tenebre (Ballett am Rhein; Lovesong (Frantic Assembly); James Son of James, The Bull, The Flowerbed (Fabulous Beast Dance Theatre); Justitia, Park (Jasmin Vardimon Dance Company); Human Shadows (Underground7; The Place Prize).**

Film includes: **Morituri Te Salutant, Baby.**

Merle works internationally in a wide variety of styles and genres. She is also a lecturer at Central St Martins School of Art and Design in London. Other teaching includes Rose Bruford College and Goldsmiths.

Jessica Hung Han Yun
(Lighting Designer)

For the Royal Court: **seven methods of killing kylie jenner, Living Newspaper, Pah-La.**

Other theatre includes: **The Mirror and the Light, Anna X (West End); Out West (Lyric, Hammersmith); She Loves Me, The Band Plays On (Crucible, Sheffield); Blindness (Donmar/UK & International tour); Inside (Orange Tree); Dick Whittington (National); Fairview (Young Vic); Equus (Theatre Royal, Stratford East/ETT/Trafalgar Studios/UK tour); Snowflake (Kiln); The Last of the Pelican Daughters (Complicité/Royal & Derngate, Northampton); Cuckoo (Soho); Armadillo (Yard); Rockets & Blue Lights (Royal Exchange, Manchester); Reasons to Stay Alive (Sheffield Theatres/ETT/UK tour);**

One (HOME, Manchester/UK tour/International tour); Summer Rolls (& Bristol Old Vic), A Pupil (Park); Faces in the Crowd, Mephisto [A Rhapsody], Dear Elizabeth, The Human Voice (Gate); Forgotten (Moongate/New Earth/Arcola/Theatre Royal, Plymouth); Hive City Legacy (Hot Brown Honey/Roundhouse); Nine Foot Nine (Bunker/Edinburgh Festival Fringe); Becoming Shades (VAULT Festival).

Dance includes: **HOME (Rambert2).**

Installation includes: **Winter Lights Installation (commissioned by Museum of the Home).**

Awards include: **Knight of Illumination Award for Plays, Off West End Award for Best Lighting Design (Equus).**

Helen Lovett Johnson
(Associate Costume Designer)

Theatre includes: **The Book of Dust (Bridge); Under Milkwood, Follies, The Hard Problem, London Road (National); Sing Street (New York Theatre Workshop); The Inheritance (Young Vic/Broadway); We Are Here (Jeremy Deller/1418 NOW); The Haunting of Hill House (Everyman, Liverpool); Sinatra (Palladium); The Same Deep Water As Me (Donmar); The Yellow Wallpaper (Schaubuhne, Berlin).**

Opera includes: **Lyssa, Die Frau Ohne Schatten (ROH); Wozzeck (Lyric Opera, Chicago); Cosi Fan Tutti, Onegin (& Metropolitan Opera), Between Worlds (ENO); Written on Skin (Festival D'Aix en Provence/ROH); Carmen (Salzburg Opera Festival).**

Dance includes: **Snow Queen, The Steadfast Tin Soldier (& HRH Queen Margerethe of Denmark), The Nutcracker (Tivoli Ballet, Copenhagen); Song of the Earth/La Sylphide, Giselle (English National Ballet); Chroma (Danish Royal Ballet); Infra (Polish National Ballet).**

Blue Makwana
(Associate Movement Director)

Blue is a London based dancer, choreographer, movement director and teacher. She teaches Contemporary and Jazz dance techniques, Musical Theatre, Commercial and Choreography in higher education vocational institutions.

Blue began her training in Ballet, Contemporary and Choreography at the Centre for Advanced Training (The CAT Programme), as well as Jazz, Musical Theatre, Modern and Tap at The BRIT School. She was also a member of the National Youth Dance Company (NYDC) where she toured a new work *In-Nocentes* around the UK. She graduated from the London Contemporary Dance School with First Class Honours in Contemporary Dance. Blue currently teaches at Bird College, The Urdang Academy, Emil Dale Academy, Trinity Laban and The Place. She has also held positions teaching and managing for

Khronos senior and youth companies at The BRIT School, EDGE Dance Company and London Contemporary Dance School. She returned to NYDC to work as an Assistant to Guest Artistic Director Alesandra Seutin on their work *Speak Volumes.*

Blue is also a dancer and Artist Assistant for Malik Nashad Sharpe aka Marikiscrycrycry, currently performing in their production *He's Dead.* Other performance credits include *Forgot To Be Your Lover* by Yukiko Masul, Burberry AW19 collection at London Fashion Week choreographed by Holly Blakey, *NEVERLAND* by Holland for GUCCI x DAZED choreographed and directed by Holly Blakey, *Mise-en-Crise* by Marikiscrycrycry and DFS *Ordinary People, Extraordinary Things* directed by Ali Kurr.

Choreographic credits include The Urdang Academy, The CAT Programme, Greenwich Docklands International Festival, Emil Dale Academy, Khronos Youth Girls and most recently as an Assistant Choreographer and Assistant Director for Malik on *Two Tracks and a Mix* for EDGE Dance Company.

Tadhg Murphy (Cast)

For the Royal Court: **Bad Roads.**

Other theatre includes: **Ballyturk (& St. Ann's Warehouse, NYC), Three Sisters (& USA tour), Aristocrats (Abbey, Dublin); Our Country's Good (National); Romeo & Juliet, Mrs. Warren's Profession, Hay Fever (& Spoleto Festival, Charleston USA), Da, The Speckled People, The Real Thing (Gate, Dublin); How These Desperate Men Talk, MedEia (Corcadorca); Waiting for Godot (Galety, Dublin/USA tour); The Cripple of Inishmaan, The Walworth Farce (& UK tour/ International tour), Penelope (Druid); The Taming of the Shrew (Rough Magic).**

Television includes: **Conversations with Friends, Brassic, The English, Red Election, Absentia, Bloodmoon, Miss Scarlett & the Duke, Counterpart, Guerrilla, Will, Black Sails, Vikings, Seachtar na Cásca, An Crisis, The Clinic, Love is the Drug, No Tears.**

Film includes: **The Northman, Wrath of Man, Dead Happy, How to Build a Girl, Undergods, Lost in the Living, Pride & Joy, Boy Eats Girl, Alexander, The Secret Market, Jelly Baby.**

Radio includes: **Relic, Vigil, The Plough & the Stars, The Finnegans, The Colleen & the Cowboy.**

Malik Nashad Sharpe
(Movement Director)

Malik is an artist working with choreography. Creating primarily underneath the alias Marikiscrycrycry, he creates performances that are formally experimental and engaged with the construction of atmosphere, affect, and dramaturgy.

Malik's works have been presented internationally and across many different contexts. UK events include Fierce Festival, *BUZZCUT* at CCA Glasgow, NOW Festival at the Yard Theatre, The Place, *Steakhouse Live* at Rich Mix, *Queer and Now* at Tate Britain, Tramway, *NottDance* at Nottingham Contemporary, Duckie, Marlborough Pub and Theatre, Theatre in the Mill, Transmission Gallery, Quarterhouse Folkestone, Attenborough Centre for Creative Arts, Cambridge Junction, London Fashion Week, Battersea Arts Centre and Institute of Contemporary Arts. Internationally, events include *American Realness*, Submerge Festival at BAC, Panoply Performance Lab and Center for Human Rights in the Arts/OSUN in the USA; Montreal arts et interculturels, Theatre La Chapelle and *Toronto Community Love-In* at Pia Bouman Theatre in Canada; Block Universe x EWerk Luckenwalde in Germany; Menagerie de Verre in France; Beursschouwburg in Belgium; and Les Urbaines Lausanne and Gessnerallee in Switzerland.

As a choreographer, he has worked with the English National Opera, Gate Theatre, Young Vic, Hampstead Theatre and at the National Theatre as a part of Summer Space to Create.

Malik is currently an associate artist at The Place and Hackney Showroom and an artist-in-residence at Sadlers Wells. He was formerly an artist-in-residence at Tate Modern, Tate Britain and at Barbican Open Labs. He is a regular contributor to Mission Statement Magazine, and his writings have been published by Vulnerable Paradoxes, MSM, MCQ, and the Capilano Review, and was recently named by Attitude Magazine as a Rising Star in Dance. He lives and makes work from London and Montreal.

Nick Powell
(Composer & Sound Designer)

For the Royal Court: **Living Newspaper, Bad Roads, The Ferryman (& West End/Broadway), X, Unreachable, The Mistress Contract, The Nether (& West End), The Ritual Slaughter of Gorge Mastromas, Talk Show, Narrative, Get Santa! [co-creator], The Vertical Hour, Relocated.**

Other theatre includes: **The Lehman Trilogy (& West End/Broadway), The Tell-Tale Heart, Othello (National); Julius Caesar (Bridge); Solar (Klangwolke, Linz); People, Places and Things (Stadsteatern, Stockholm); City of Glass (59 Productions); Alice in Wonderland (Lyceum, Edinburgh); Peter Pan, All My Sons, Lord of the Flies, The Crucible (Regent's Park Open Air/UK tour); Lanark: A Life in Three Acts (& Citizens, Glasgow), 27, The Wheel, The Wonderful World of Dissocia (& National Theatre of Scotland); Realism (Edinburgh International Festival); Dunsinane (& tour), A Life of Galileo, Richard III, The Drunks, God in Ruins (RSC); Urtain, Marat-Sade, Los Macbez (CDN, Madrid); Paradise (Rhurtriennale, Germany); 'Tis Pity She's a Whore (Cheek by Jowl); Penumbra,**

Tito Andronico (Animalario, Madrid); The Wolves in the Walls (& National Theatre of Scotland/New Victory, NYC/UK tour); Panic (Improbable); Wolf Hall/Bring Up the Bodies [as sound designer] (RSC/West End/Broadway).

Awards include: Drama Desk Award for Outstanding Sound Design of a Play (The Ferryman); Spanish Premio Max for Best Musical Composition for Scenic Arts (Urtain).

Nick also writes for TV and film, and is half of OSKAR, who have made two albums, numerous installations, and live soundtracks for Prada, Milan. In 2017, he scored *Bloom*, Edinburgh International Festival's opening event and the Guggenheim Museum, Bilbao's 20th anniversary celebration *Reflections*. His chamber piece *Cold Calling: The Arctic Project* was presented at the Birmingham Rep with the City of Birmingham Symphony Orchestra in 2016 and he was music consultant on Sam Mendes' *1917*. His debut solo album *Walls Fall Down* was released in 2021.

Tal Rosner (Video Designer)

For the Royal Court: You For Me For You, X.

Other theatre includes: Brothers Lionheart (Royal Danish Playhouse, Copenhagen); Everyman, Husbands & Sons (National); Shopping & F***ing [co-designer] (Lyric, Hammersmith); Camp Siegfried (Old Vic).

Dance includes: The Most Incredible Thing (Charlotte Ballet, North Carolina); Les Enfants Terribles (Royal Ballet); 8 Minutes [co-creator] (Sadler's Wells).

Opera includes: Die Walküre [co-director] (Opéra National de Bordeaux).

Installations include: Steve Reich's Tehillim (Psalms) (commissioned by the Barbican Centre); Olga Neuwirth's Disenchanted Island (commissioned by IRCAM and Centre Pompidou); Lament [co-creator] (commissioned by Nuit Blanche Toronto).

Orchestral work includes: MYTHOS [director] (commissioned by Staatsoper Hannover); Foreign Bodies (commissioned by the New York Philharmonic); Four Sea Interludes, Passacaglia (New World Symphony/San Francisco Symphony/Los Angeles Philharmonic/Philadelphia Orchestra/BBC Symphony Orchestra); In Seven Days (Piano Concerto with Moving Image) (commissioned by the Southbank Centre/Los Angeles Philharmonic).

Awards include: BAFTA for Best Title Sequence (Skins).

Tal is an artist and creative director working closely with musicians, theatre makers and fashion brands, combining multiple layers of sound and visuals to create video installations and live performances. In the commercial arena, Tal has creatively directed the video content for Louis Vuitton's traveling exhibit *Time Capsule* as well as LVX in Beverly Hills, The Pet Shop Boys' *Super Tour* (worldwide) and the Rolling Stones' *No Filter* European Tour.

In 2020 he directed the video element in Marni's *MARNIFESTO*, which took its SS21 collection out to the world and streamed globally to an audience of over 20,000; and has collaborated with NYC collective TELFAR on their SS20 runway show at Paris Fashion Week and AW20 installation at Pitti Uomo, Florence.

Rosie Thackeray
(Assistant Director)

As director, theatre includes: EAST (Edinburgh Festival Fringe).

As assistant director, theatre includes: Amal Meets Alice – The Walk (Good Chance, Story Museum).

As movement director, theatre includes: WE WON'T FALL (Switch MCR).

Rosie is alumni of the Royal Exchange's Young Company and the Royal Court's Agitator programmes.

Bret Yount (Fight Director)

For the Royal Court: Cyprus Avenue (& Abbey, Dublin/Public, NYC), The Cane, Linda, Violence & Son, The Low Road, In Basildon, Wastwater, No Quarter, Belong, Remembrance Day, Redbud, Spur of the Moment, The Nether (& West End).

Other theatre includes: Top Girls, Nine Night, Ma Rainey's Black Bottom, Treasure Island, A Taste of Honey, Emil & the Detectives, The World of Extreme Happiness, Double Feature, Moon on a Rainbow Shawl, Men Should Weep (National); City of Angels, Caroline or Change, Foxfinder, Red Velvet, The Winter's Tale/Harlequinade, American Buffalo, Bad Jews, Fences, Posh, Absent Friends, Death & the Maiden, Clybourne Park, The Harder They Come, The Lover/The Collection (West End); Richard III, Private Lives (UK tour); Waiting for Godot, Romeo & Juliet, The Effect (Crucible, Sheffield); The Winter's Tale (Cheek by Jowl); A Very Expensive Poison, The Hairy Ape (Old Vic); Nine Night, The Wasp (Trafalgar Studios); The One, Blueberry Toast, First Love is the Revolution (Soho); Hamlet (Barbican); Richard II, The Tempest, Much Ado About Nothing, Romeo & Juliet, Anne Boleyn (Globe); Medea (Gate); Tipping the Velvet (Lyric, Hammersmith); The Pirates of Penzance, La Traviata, The Mastersingers of Nuremberg, La Fanciulla, Benvenuto Cellini, Rodelinda (ENO); King Lear, The Merchant of Venice, Arden of Faversham, The Roaring Girl, Wolf Hall/Bring Up the Bodies, Candide (RSC); 'Tis Pity She's a Whore, The Broken Heart (Sam Wanamaker Playhouse); Teenage Dick, Europe, Appropriate, Splendour, Roots, City of Angels, The Physicists, The Recruiting Officer (Donmar); All My Sons, Cannibals, Orpheus Descending (Royal Exchange, Manchester); The Trial,

A Streetcar Named Desire, A Season in the Congo, Public Enemy (Young Vic); Ghosts (& Trafalgar Studios/BAM, NYC), Chimerica (& West End), Children's Children, The Knot of the Heart, House of Games, Ruined (Almeida); The Norman Conquests, A Streetcar Named Desire, Macbeth, The Caretaker, Lost Monsters (Liverpool Playhouse/Everyman, Liverpool); Dangerous Lady, Shalom, Baby, A Clockwork Orange – The Musical, The Graft, Two Women, Gladiator Games, Bashment (Theatre Royal, Stratford East).

Television includes: **Quick Cuts, Against All Odds, Blue Peter.**

Film includes: **Troy.**

Ria Zmitrowicz (Cast)

For the Royal Court: **Gundog, Bad Roads, X.**

Other theatre includes: **The Welkin (National); The Doctor, Three Sisters, Dance Nation (Almeida); Plastic (Theatre Royal, Bath); Four Minutes Twelve Seconds (Trafalgar Studios/Hampstead); The Crucible (Royal Exchange, Manchester); Arcadia (ETT); God's Property (Soho); Chapel Street (Bush/Old Red Lion); Skanky (Arcola).**

Television includes: **The Power, The Third Day Live: Autumn, On The Edge, Three Girls, Mr Selfridge, Youngers, Nightshift, The Midnight Beast, Murder on the Home Front, Whitechapel.**

Film includes: **Misbehaviour, Teen Spirit, Puppy [short], Kill Your Friends.**

THE ROYAL COURT THEATRE

The Royal Court Theatre is the writers' theatre. It is a leading force in world theatre for cultivating and supporting writers – undiscovered, emerging and established.

Through the writers, the Royal Court is at the forefront of creating restless, alert, provocative theatre about now. We open our doors to the unheard voices and free thinkers that, through their writing, change our way of seeing.

Over 120,000 people visit the Royal Court in Sloane Square, London, each year and many thousands more see our work elsewhere through transfers to the West End and New York, UK and international tours, digital platforms, our residencies across London, and our site-specific work. Through all our work we strive to inspire audiences and influence future writers with radical thinking and provocative discussion.

The Royal Court's extensive development activity encompasses a diverse range of writers and artists and includes an ongoing programme of writers' attachments, readings, workshops and playwriting groups. Twenty years of the International Department's pioneering work around the world means the Royal Court has relationships with writers on every continent.

Since 1956 we have commissioned and produced hundreds of writers, from John Osborne to Jasmine Lee-Jones. Royal Court plays from every decade are now performed on stage and taught in classrooms and universities across the globe.

We're now working to the future and are committed to becoming carbon net zero and ensuring we are a just, equitable, transparent and ethical cultural space - from our anti-oppression work, to our relationship with freelancers, to credible climate pledges.

It is because of this commitment to the writer and our future that we believe there is no more important theatre in the world than the Royal Court.

Find out more at royalcourttheatre.com

 royalcourt   royalcourttheatre

Supported using public funding by
ARTS COUNCIL ENGLAND

ROYAL COURT SUPPORTERS

The Royal Court relies on its supporters in addition to our core grant from Arts Council England and our ticket sales. We are particularly grateful to the individuals, trusts and companies who stood by us and continued to support our work during these recent difficult times. It is with this vital support that the Royal Court remains the writers' theatre and that we can continue to seek out, develop and nurture new voices, both on and off our stages.

Thank you to all who support the Royal Court in this way. We really can't do it without you.

PUBLIC FUNDING

 Supported using public funding by
ARTS COUNCIL ENGLAND

CHARITABLE PARTNERS

BackstageTrust

JERWOOD ARTS

ORANGE TREE TRUST

CORPORATE SPONSORS

Aqua Financial Ltd
Cadogan
Colbert
Edwardian Hotels, London
SISTER

CORPORATE MEMBERS

Platinum
Auriens
Bloomberg Philanthropies

Silver
Left Bank Pictures
Patrizia
Sloane Stanley

TRUSTS & FOUNDATIONS

The Derrill Allatt Foundation
The Backstage Trust
Martin Bowley Charitable Trust
The City Bridge Trust
The Cleopatra Trust
Cockayne – Grants for the Arts
The Noël Coward Foundation
Cowley Charitable Foundation
The D'Oyly Carte Charitable Trust
Edgerton Foundation
Garrick Charitable Trust
The Golden Bottle Trust
Roderick & Elizabeth Jack
Jerwood Arts
Kirsh Foundation
The London Community Foundation
Clare McIntyre's Bursary
Lady Antonia Fraser for the Pinter Commission
Old Possum's Practical Trust
Richard Radcliffe Charitable Trust
Rose Foundation
Royal Victoria Hall Foundation
The Charles Skey Charitable Trust
John Thaw Foundation
Thistle Trust
The Victoria Wood Foundation

To find out more about supporting the Royal Court please get in touch with the Development Team at support@royalcourttheatre.com, call 020 7565 5030 or visit royalcourttheatre.com/support-us

ROYAL

BAR & KITCHEN

The Royal Court's Bar & Kitchen aims to create a welcoming and inspiring environment with a style and ethos that reflects the work we put on stage.

Offering expertly crafted cocktails alongside an extensive selection of craft gins and beers, wine and soft drinks, our vibrant basement bar provides a sanctuary in the middle of Sloane Square. By day a perfect spot for meetings or quiet reflection and by night atmospheric meeting spaces for cast, crew, audiences and the general public.

All profits go directly to supporting the work of the Royal Court theatre, cultivating and supporting writers – undiscovered, emerging and established.

For more information, visit
royalcourttheatre.com/bar

HIRES & EVENTS

The Royal Court is available to hire for celebrations, rehearsals, meetings, filming, ceremonies and much more. Our two theatre spaces can be hired for conferences and showcases, and the building is a unique venue for bespoke events and receptions.

For more information, visit
royalcourttheatre.com/events

Sloane Square London, SW1W 8AS ⊖ Sloane Square ⇌ Victoria Station
🐦 royalcourt 📘 theroyalcourttheatre 📷 royalcourttheatre

COURT

SUPPORT THE COURT AND BE A PART OF OUR FUTURE.

Every penny raised goes directly towards producing bold new writing for our stages, cultivating and supporting writers in the UK and around the world, and inspiring the next generation of theatre-makers.

You can make a one-off donation by text:

Text **Support 5** to 70560 to donate £5

Text **Support 10** to 70560 to donate £10

Text **Support 20** to 70560 to donate £20

Texts cost the donation amount plus one standard message. UK networks only.

To find out more about the different ways in which you can get involved, visit our website: royalcourttheatre.com/support-us

The English Stage Company at the Royal Court Theatre is a registered charity (No. 231242)

The Glow

for Robert Holman,
who lit the way.

Cast of Characters

The Woman

Mrs Lyall
Mason

Haster

All other characters to be played by the performers playing
Mrs Lyall, Mason, and Haster (see appendix).

To be played on an almost bare stage,
as much as possible conjured through light and shadow.

Notes.

A question without a question mark denotes a flatness of tone.

- Indicates an interruption of speech or train of thought.
… Indicates either a trailing off, a breather, a shift, or a
transition.
/ Indicates where the next line of dialogue interrupts or
overlaps.
{ } Contains dialogue not heard by the audience.

I:
A Prominent Woman.

1.
1863.
An asylum. A cell without windows.
The Woman *sits on the ground, a shape in the shadows.*
Mrs Lyall *stands holding a lantern, the only source of light.*

Silence.

Mrs Lyall *lifts the lantern–*
The Woman *retreats slightly as the light touches her.*

Pause.

Mrs Lyall   Would you mind my taking a step closer?
So I might let the light find you?

Pause.

Mrs Lyall *moves to sit by* **The Woman**, *who retreats a little more.*

Mrs Lyall   Now now–
You've no need to be afraid.
…
Let's have a look at you–

She brings her hands to **The Woman's** *face and inspects her.*

Mrs Lyall   …I wonder.
Yes, I wonder what we might find under all of this.

She produces a handkerchief and begins wiping the grime from **The Woman's** *face.*

Mrs Lyall   Well now.
One wouldn't expect to find such a pretty young thing down
here in the dark.

...

Do you have any idea as to how long you've been here?

The Woman ...*(Shakes head.)*

Mrs Lyall Or perhaps who brought you here in the first?

The Woman ...*(Shakes head.)*

Mrs Lyall Are you receiving any treatment at all?

The Woman ...

Mrs Lyall Do the doctors or the porters come down here to see you?

The Woman *(Shakes head.)*

Beat.

Mrs Lyall Well how about a name.

The Woman ...

Mrs Lyall You must have a name, at the very least. That's something we're all given.

The Woman ...

Mrs Lyall ...Well how terrible for you.

Pause.

Mrs Lyall *drops the handkerchief to the ground.*

Mrs Lyall My name-

Is Mrs Evelyn Lyall.

I am a prominent woman.

I am a writer, a social thinker, and a spiritualist medium of some renown.

And do you know-

Despite these achievements,

My own husband once tried to have me locked in a room very like this one.

So perhaps we're not so different, you and I.

…

Do you have any understanding, as to what a spiritualist medium is?

The Woman   …*(Shakes head.)*

Mrs Lyall   Well-

There is the world of matter- That which is seen.

And the world of the spirit- That which remains unseen by the great majority.

A medium conducts explorations into the latter.

…

I've come here in the course of my work.

And I feel so fortunate to have found you.

Do you know why?

The Woman   *(Shakes head.)*

Mrs Lyall *stands.*

Mrs Lyall   It has become clear to me that I am in need of an assistant.

I require a young, passive woman to amplify my own mediumship further.

I've spent the entire night searching this hospital for a suitable candidate and found none.

But now here we are.

...
Would you like to come home with me?

2.
The Lyall House, by candlelight.
Mrs Lyall *and* **Mason**.
Sadie *(The Woman) stands nearby, in the gloom.*

Mason   For how long?

Mrs Lyall   For as long as our work together requires.

Mason   Your 'work' requires she *live* here.
Even your coven would baulk at the very idea-

Mrs Lyall   I have disbanded my previous circle.

Mason   You repulsed them with your unsavoury obsessions.

Mrs Lyall   They lacked ambition.

Pause.

Mason   So this girl replaces them.

Mrs Lyall   And you shall join us.

Beat.

Mason   Absolutely not.

Mrs Lyall   That was not a request, Mason.

Mason   I won't collaborate in your sickness-

Mrs Lyall   The circle must be at least three.

Mason   So go drag another from the hole you found this one.
Better still, open the doors and invite the mudlarks in-

Mrs Lyall   I won't debate with you.

Mason   And I won't live with some filthy woman you found in
the gutter-
(To **Sadie***.)* Don't *look* at me, Girl-

She looks at the floor.

Mrs Lyall   I'll trust you not to be unkind to her.

Mason   I will be as unkind as I like.
Do you think Father will approve of this?

Mrs Lyall   I take no interest in your father's opinions.

Mason   He'll set to having you-

Mrs Lyall   If you share his beliefs you are welcome to follow
him in seeking alternate accommodation.
It will of course mean a reduction in your allowance.

Mason   …

Mrs Lyall *turns to* **Sadie**.

Mrs Lyall   Mason will take you to your room now.

Mason   I removed the cot from the scullery.

Mrs Lyall   She will sleep in the room adjacent to mine.

Mason   That's my room-

Mrs Lyall   You may move your belongings to the third floor.

Mason   …

Mrs Lyall   *(To* **Sadie**.*)* Good night, my darling.
Pay no mind to Mason's behaviours, you are very welcome here.

Mrs Lyall *leaves.*

Silence.

Mason *stares at* **Sadie**.

Eventually he snatches a candlestick from a table.

Mason   Come along then.

He goes to leave. **Sadie** *remains.*

Mason   Come *along.*

She hurries after him as he leads her through hallways, upstairs, and down hallways darker still.

Mason   I shall move my possessions from the room tomorrow; if you touch any of them I shall beat you.
When morning comes, do not open the shutters.
Like all ghouls my mother insists on darkness.
Now the servants have been dismissed doubtless *I* shall be expected to prepare your meals.
I have no interest in your preferences, you will eat what you are given.

He stops and turns to face her.

Mason   This is not your home.
When Mother tires of you she shall toss you back where you
were found.
Until then you stay out of my way, do you understand?
…
Are you *listening*, Girl?

Sadie   Yyeesss-

Beat.

Sadie *looks quickly to her feet, unnerved by the cracked bark of her voice.*

Mason *stares at her a moment longer before removing a candle from the
stick and thrusting it at her.*

Mason   Here.
Down the hall.

He leaves.

Sadie *stands alone in the dim light of the candle.*

She looks around.

She makes her way slowly down the hall, feeling her way.

We listen to her nervous breathing.

We hear a heavy footstep nearby-

Another-

Someone is approaching in the dark.

Sadie *lifts the candle and watches as a* **Knight** *in bloodied armour steps into the light.*

They consider each other.

The candle goes out.

3.
Mrs Lyall *lights a candle. There is a table without chairs.*
Sadie *stands nearby.*

Mrs Lyall   Sadie.

Sadie *is distracted, looking off and away.*

Mrs Lyall   Sadie.

Sadie   Yes.

Mrs Lyall   You're not yet used to your new name.
Is it clear what's expected of you this evening.

Sadie   …

Mrs Lyall   I don't relish repeating myself, Sadie.

Sadie   I hearrdd voices.

Mrs Lyall   Voices. Whose voices?

Sadie   I donn't…
…
I don'tt-

Enter **Mason**.

Mason   I refuse to cook for her.
She wouldn't touch a thing I prepared.

Mrs Lyall   Perhaps if you prepared something edible, Mason.

Mason   It's not enough you give her my room, you'll have me
serve as her *maid-*

Mrs Lyall   That's quite enough theatrics for now.
I must retire to calibrate myself and quiet is essential whilst I do
so.
Imagine the volume I might prefer your voice to be at, then
lower it still.

Mrs Lyall *leaves.*

Mason   …an evening with my mother and the dead.
How did my social life plunge to such depths.

Sadie *watches as* **Mason** *pours himself a drink.*

Mason   I don't like being stared at, Girl.

Sadie   …wwerre you aafrraidd?

Mason   Is your tongue as slow as the rest of you?

Sadie   …

Mason   Afraid of what.

Sadie   The ffirst timme Mrs Lyall-
Ttethered your ssoul to herrs.

Mason   My mother never 'tethered her soul' to mine.
Parents traditionally don't use their children in demonic rituals.
Did your own ever use you to raise the dead?

Sadie   I ddon't remember. My parents.

Mason   I imagine you would had they shared my mother's
interests.

Sadie   …I-

Mason   What is that.

Sadie   …

Mason   What are you fiddling with there.

Sadie   …

Mason   Show me.

Sadie   …

Mason   *Show* me.

Sadie *has a small stuffed horse.*

Pause.

Mason   …Give that to me.

Sadie   …

Mason   It is mine. Give it to me.

Sadie   I ffffound it-

Mason   In my room. Give it here.

Sadie   ...

Mason   *Give* it.

Sadie   No.

Beat.

Mason *strides across the room and snatches the horse.*

Sadie   No-

Mason   Did I not tell you to leave my belongings untouched?
Are you *deaf*?
You touch my things again and I'll have you replaced with some
other damaged girl-

Mrs Lyall *has returned in a new dress.*

Mrs Lyall   Mason, I won't have you bullying her.

Mason   She is *stealing* from me-

Mrs Lyall   What use can you have for that old thing?

Mason   She stole my room and now she steals my possessions-

Mrs Lyall   If she wants it for company at night what harm
can that-
Mason-

Mason *has ripped the horse in two and throw the pieces to the ground.*

Mason   There. Now there are no jealousies.

He goes to leave-

Mrs Lyall   Mason really- *Mason*.
We are ready to begin.

Sadie *is inspecting the torn horse.*

Mrs Lyall   You will make peace with Sadie and clear this atmosphere.
The spirits favour a light, welcoming air.

Mason   Then they would do well to visit another house.

Mrs Lyall   Now come along.

Mason   ...She's staring at me.

Sadie's *eyes are fixed coldly on* **Mason**.

Mrs Lyall   Mason was acting out in a juvenile manner, we shan't take it to heart, shall we Sadie.

Sadie *continues to stare.*
Something is shifting in the room's atmosphere.

Mason   Stop-
Looking at me like that-

Mrs Lyall   Besides, you're a grown woman. You've no need for a child's toy, have you.
Have you, Sadie.

Mason   Tell her to stop.
...
/Stop- Stop this-

Mrs Lyall   Sadie.
…
Sadie.

Sadie *turns away and goes to* **Mrs Lyall's** *side.*

Mrs Lyall   There.

Mason   Did you see how she looked at me-

Mrs Lyall   We are moving on with our evening.

Mason   She-

Mrs Lyall · Mason you will take your place at the piano
without further complaint.

Beat.

Mason *retreats to a piano in the corner of the room.*
Mrs Lyall *takes* **Sadie's** *hand.*

Mrs Lyall   Now Sadie, you are excused from singing of
course until you become familiar with the words. For now, just
try and contribute to a bright, positive aura.
Are we ready?

Mason *starts playing.*

Mrs Lyall   There we are.

Mrs Lyall *begins to sing-*

　　　　　　　Only a thin veil between us-

Mrs Lyall   I shan't be a lone voice-

Mason *joins-*

> My loved ones so precious and true-

Mrs Lyall   If you could find a little more enthusiasm-

> Only as mist before sunrise,
> I am hidden away from your view-

Mrs Lyall   *Much* better- Maintaining this level-

> Often I come with my blessing,
> And strive all your sorrows to share-

Sadie *becomes distracted as a strange echo laps at the walls.*

> At night when you're quietly sleeping,
> I kiss down your eyelids in prayer-

Soon, it's as if the scene has been plunged underwater.

Mrs Lyall   And onto the chorus-

She looks up as the sound of a bird calling breaks through the fog.

> Only a thin veil between us,
> Some morning the angels will come,
> And then in a bright land of beauty-
> We'll gather with loved ones at home,
> At home-

Just as she's about to panic, the scene rushes back to the surface, and **Sadie** *joins in with the song, her voice a manic yell-*

Mrs Lyall *and* **Mason** *gradually stop singing and playing to watch her.*

Home, beautiful home,
No longer in sadness alone,
But safe, in the kingdom of glory,
We'll dwell, with the loved ones at home-

Pause.

Mrs Lyall   That's-
Very good, Sadie.
…
You should have mentioned you knew the words.

Pause.

Mrs Lyall   If I could ask you to take your place.

Sadie *clambers up onto the table and lies down.*
Mrs Lyall *moves to the head of the table, placing her hands around* **Sadie's** *skull.*

Mrs Lyall   Mason.

Mason *moves to the other end of the table.*
He reluctantly takes hold of **Sadie's** *feet.*

Mrs Lyall   And now we'll make it known to whomever might be present here this evening that you are welcome, and that we await any communication you might send us with patience and open arms.
And Sadie, as we discussed- You will clear your mind and allow yourself to become completely passive whilst we wait.

Mason   An irony that your power is to render yourself powerless.

Mrs Lyall   Thank you, Mason.

Sadie   MMMrs Lyalll-

Mrs Lyall   Hush now, Sadie.

Mrs Lyall *settles in for a long wait.*

A long time passes.

A clock in the next room chimes the hour.

A long time passes.

A long time.

Mason   ...How much longer must we-

A loud thump from somewhere. **Mason** *jumps.*

Mrs Lyall   Here we are.

Sadie *seems uneasy.*

Mrs Lyall   Good evening to you, Spirit.
If you would bear with me whilst we establish a simple system
of communication-

If we could agree on a single rap for a 'yes' and two raps for a 'no', would that be acceptable to you?

Pause.

A thump. Softer, this time.

Mrs Lyall   Splendid.
Are you alone this evening?

Pause.

Another thump. Softer, still.

Mrs Lyall   Very good.
Are you a former tenant of this house?

Pause.

Two thumps.

Mrs Lyall   No. Then-

Another-

Mrs Lyall   No-
If you could try and keep to the system /we agreed-

Mason   How are you doing that?

Mrs Lyall   Quiet-

Mason   Where is it coming from?

Mrs Lyall   *Quiet-*

Sadie   Mmrs Lyall-

Mrs Lyall   Did you pass-

Sadie   I cann'tt-

Mrs Lyall   Did you pass before your time-

A very long scraping of fingernails on board-

A moment.

Then a colossal bang-

Sadie *is hyperventilating.*

Mrs Lyall   Sadie-

Mason   What is this?

An extremely loud thump-

Mason   Mother, stop-

Mrs Lyall   Rest, spirit, rest-

More thumps, scraping, louder-

Mrs Lyall   How might we converse if you insist on-

Silence.

A long scream pulls out of **Sadie**-
Starved of oxygen at first, it rises from a rasp to a roar-
She leaps up from the table, thrashing-

Mrs Lyall   Hold her- *Hold her-* The Spirit has her-

They try and restrain **Sadie** *as the crashing continues, louder-*

Mrs Lyall   *Hold* her Mason-

Mason   I'm /trying-

Sadie   meam lucem demere conantur- meam lucem demere conantur!

4.
Mason *is watching the front of the house from an upstairs window.*
The last of the day's light crosses the room through the open shutter.

Enter **Mrs Lyall***.*

Mrs Lyall   Have they left.

The bell rings downstairs.

Mrs Lyall   …How many are they.

Mason   Two. And a third with the carriage.

Pause.

Mason   They're leaving.

Pause.

Mason *comes away from the window.*

Mason   Who is she?

Mrs Lyall   She is nobody. She means nothing to no one.

Mason   Clearly that's not the case if they're sending men to retrieve her.

Mrs Lyall   They held no record of her even being there. She was abandoned in an unused cell. I doubt she'd seen another for years.

Mason   Someone must have been feeding her-

Mrs Lyall   She is *no* one.

Mason   Then send her back and find another-

Mrs Lyall   Absolutely not. I paid more than handsomely for her-

Mason   You paid a porter for silence whilst you stole her-

Mrs Lyall   I did not 'steal' anything-

Mason   You can find another.
One more tolerable to live with-
One who doesn't talk to herself at all hours- Spend all night clattering about in the library-

Mrs Lyall   You have made your dislike for her clear.

Mason   Any number of women can perform your table rappings for you-

Mrs Lyall   You would call what I brought to pass table rappings?

Pause.

Mrs Lyall   Sadie is a perfect conduit for my powers.
I could never hope to find another as attuned.
I brought a spirit *into* her body.
You heard how she spoke.

Mason   She spoke in Latin. She is performing for you, to stay in your favour-

Mrs Lyall   How could she know such a language?
Without education?

Mason   You don't know what education she has-
You don't know anything about her-

Mrs Lyall   What did she say.

Beat.

Mason   …I failed Latin.

Mrs Lyall   I am aware of your failures, Mason.

Pause.

Mason   Light.
…something about- Stealing her light.

Pause.

Mrs Lyall   They are not coming for her.
Your father's lifestyle has once again extended beyond what I give him.
He has likely begun a second campaign to have me removed from control of my accounts.

Mason   So stop these acts which give him fuel to-

Mrs Lyall   You might sooner ask I stop breathing.
What I could have achieved by now, had so much of my time
not been spent hiding money from men.
I am about to make all distinctions of flesh irrelevant.
To birth the new age of the spirit.
I will not allow small-mindedness to threaten that.
…
And if it be the case they are pursuing her, soon there will be no
one left to claim.
I shall fill Sadie with the ancient spirit of another in
*per*manence.
What little there is of her shall be erased.
Then your father and any others intent on containing me will
kneel before me.
…
They cannot lock away a proven necromancer.

Pause.

Mrs Lyall   I can smell the drink on you.
I need your wits sharp.

Mrs Lyall *leaves.*

Mason *mops his brow.*

Sadie *is stood in the shadows, holding a book.*

Mason *sees her and jumps.*

Mason   How long have you been standing there?
…
Go to your room.

Sadie   What's wrong with you?

Mason   Nothing. Nothing is wrong with me.
A fine question for *you* to ask.

He closes the window shutter.

Sadie   Who was outside?

Mason   No one.

Sadie   You were talking about me.

Beat.

Mason   You think we have nothing better to discuss than you?
Go to your room, you'll need rest if you're to perform tonight.

Sadie   I don't want to do it again.

Mason   I dare say it's not up to us.

Sadie   It hurts.

Mason   You don't need to maintain your act around me.
…
What are you clutching-

He snatches her book.

Sadie   Poems-

Mason   Tennyson. Knights and grails and nonsense.
A little advanced for you, isn't it?
Last I knew you were reading fairy tales.

Sadie   Give it back now.

Mason   This quest of yours for education is a waste of time.
One can dress a dog in finery- It is still a dog.
All night I hear you talking to yourself in the library-
Don't you sleep?

Pause.

Mason   You don't sleep?

Pause.

Mason   …You don't sleep.

Pause.

Sadie   Give my book back now.

Pause.

Mason   It is not 'your' book.
You do not own any books.
You own nothing.
You are squatting in my home. Reading *my* books.
Taking advantage of *my* mother's desperation to-
I *told* you-

Sadie *is reaching for the book-*
Mason *grabs her wrist-*

There's a flash, and we're suddenly on a scorched battlefield, the ground soaked with blood. Fires blaze nearby.
We make out the shadows of warring men, the cries of fury and pain.

Mason *looks around in panic-*
He lets go of **Sadie's** *wrist-*

Instantly we're back in the Lyall house.

Pause.

Mason *stares at* **Sadie**, *who is breathing heavily.*
He drops the book and flees.

Sadie *recovers herself.*

She picks the book up and clamps it to her chest, muttering to herself inaudibly.

Sadie *continues to whisper.*
We only catch occasional words.

She hears something and looks off-

She puts the book down and walks towards the sound, away from the candlelight.

We listen to her whispering as she walks.

The sounds of wildlife as dull light creeps through a canopy of leaves-

We are in a forest.

Sadie   {-and when riding across the land he meets a woman on a shining white horse come away come away she called to him and her beauty was so great he fell in deepest love and climbed onto the back of her horse and they rode across the fields and the hills until they reached the sea and kept riding until they rode across the surface of the water and under the waves to a magical kingdom where all was well where there were no wars and no disease and they were married and lived happily together-}

A **Man** *in animal hides is hunched in the dirt, his back to her.*

He turns and sees her.

He stands, clutching a rock.

He looks her up and down.

He steps towards her-

> **Sadie** *reaches out her hand-*
> *A bright spark of light ignites in her palm, hovering.*

The **Man** *stops and stares at it, fearful.*

Pause.

Sadie *is seized from behind by* **Aulus**, *a Roman Soldier-*

The spark dies, the **Man** *and the forest vanish-*

Sadie *struggles with* **Aulus** *as he tries to restrain her-*

Aulus   noli te moveri-

Sadie *manages to get on top of* **Aulus** *and wrap her hands around his skull-*

We begin to hear a voice from somewhere-

Mrs Lyall   *(From off.)* Sadie…

Aulus *grunts in pain as* **Sadie's** *fingers push into his flesh-*

Mrs Lyall   *(From off.)* Sadie-

Sadie   ego sum lux-!

She leans down and rips **Aulus'** *nose away with her teeth, spitting it out-*
Blood sprays as he yells-

Mrs Lyall   Spirit- Release!

Mrs Lyall *pulls* **Sadie** *away from* **Mason** *as he screams and clutches his face-*

Sadie *looks on with horror as* **Mason** *flees the room.*

Sadie   I saw him...

Mrs Lyall   That's alright, my darling.

Sadie   I saw him-

Mrs Lyall   Don't fret now-
My clever darling...
My clever girl...

Mrs Lyall *cradles* **Sadie**, *stroking her hair.*

5.
Mrs Lyall *cradles* **Sadie** *in a dim pool of candlelight.*

Mrs Lyall   To think the condition I found you in-
And now look at you.
Part of the most important work of the century.

Sadie   I hurt him...

Mrs Lyall   Mason will recover.

Sadie   I thought he was someone else...

Mrs Lyall   You are so passive the spirits will flock to you.
It can be overwhelming.
Be assured I am in control the entire time.

Sadie   I don't think they're spirits.

Beat.

Mrs Lyall   Well you are uneducated in these matters. You shall trust my judgement.

Sadie   Feels like- Hands.
In my skull.
And I see things.

Mrs Lyall   What do you see.

Sadie   I can't make sense of it.

Mrs Lyall   Let me help you.

Pause.

Sadie   …blood.
…pain.
…
Holes in the ground filled with the dead.
Men hung flaming on chains.
People spread open on the ground.
…
I see myself at the head of a great army.
Stood on a battlefield soaked with ruin.
I see them all at once from a great height.
Piled up. Piles. Bloated. Rotted. Looking-
Looking at me.
Pulling at my feet.
Wanting things from me.
And I can't give them what they want.
So they hate me.
And I hate them.

Even you.
Sometimes I look at you and I hate you, too.
You're the same as the rest.

Pause.

Mrs Lyall   I don't want anything from you, Sadie.

Sadie   Yes you do.

Pause.

Mrs Lyall   I want to help you.
To elevate you.
I want to water you until you bloom.
…
These are dreams. Phantoms.
Perhaps there are parts of your past muddled amongst them,
but what does it matter?
You are here with me now.
None of it matters.
Aren't you happy here?

Sadie   …

Mrs Lyall   You are in a rare position in life.
Most people are so terribly alone.
It is a grotesque fate to be born human.
Trapped within one's self in a cage of flesh.
…
You and I are forging a bond to transcend that curse.
Our spirits shall be twinned.
Stitched together with cords of brilliant light.
Doesn't that sound wonderful?

Sadie   …I want to know who I am.

Mrs Lyall   You are my darling Sadie.

Whoever you were before is an irrelevance.

I named you anew, and soon I shall gift you a new soul to match.

This person you have been has brought you nothing but pain.

We shall replace her with another.

So you might have a new life.

And when the world knows me as the woman who tore the veil between worlds, my power shall be absolute.

And you will be there by my side.

My spirit daughter.

Beat.

Mason *bursts in, drunk. Where his nose was is now a bloody hole.*

Mason   If you require dinner I shan't be making any.

Mrs Lyall   Mason you will bandage yourself, I won't have you dripping throughout the sitting.

Mason   You won't have to suffer my presence at all this evening Mother, I shall not be participating.

Mrs Lyall   You're drunk.

Mason   Not half as much as I'd care to be.

Mrs Lyall   I ask so little of you-

Mason   You ask the *Earth*.

You ask I share my home with this thing-

Sadie   Don't call me that-

Mason   You ask I tolerate being *mutilated*-

Mrs Lyall   Such melodrama-

Mason   *Look* at me.
I could charge ad*mission* for this.

Sadie   I didn't mean to- I thought you were someone else-

Mrs Lyall   /You see?

Mason   *Who?!* Who did you think I was?!
…
I won't work in your morgue a minute longer-

Mrs Lyall   I shan't allow your cowardice to stall my progress-
My powers will not be suppressed-

Mason   You *have* no powers.

Pause.

Mason   You're a fraud.
The worst kind of fraud. Unaware you are one.
There is no such thing as a spiritual medium.
…
It's her.
…
She-
Is…Something.

Pause.

Mason   She doesn't eat. She doesn't sleep.
She causes- *Things* to occur-

Mrs Lyall   That's enough.

Mason   She is something *other*.
You should never have brought her into this house.
She was locked away for a reason.

…

You see how she looks at me?

Mrs Lyall   We are both looking at you with displeasure.

Pause.

Mason *grabs* **Sadie** *by her clothing-*

Sadie   /Let go-

Mrs Lyall   Mason-

Mason   If you refuse to evict her, I shall do it for you-

Mrs Lyall   /Put her down-

Sadie   Let go of me-

Mason   She's lucky I'm being so lenient- We should burn her at the stake-!

Sadie *pushes her finger into* **Mason's** *wound-*
As he screams she presses her face to his-

Mason *vanishes.*

Silence.

Mrs Lyall *walks about the room, then off, looking for* **Mason**.
Sadie *stands stock still, breathing heavily.*

Mrs Lyall *returns.*

Pause.

The Woman   I sent him away.

Pause.

Mrs Lyall   Sadie-

The Woman   I won't help you anymore.

Mrs Lyall   You are to wait for my instruction before conducting any-

The Woman   I know who I am.

Pause.

The Woman   I saw-

Mrs Lyall   You are nothing, Sadie.
…
You are waste.
Thrown away like spoiled meat.
Your sole value is the role I have given you.
You are a tool for my using. An empty vessel I will fill however I choose.
…
But now you're convinced of your importance, is that it?
You perform one crude vanishing act and think you can usurp me?
You are a woman of great significance.
To be feared.

Pause.

Mrs Lyall *strides across the room and seizes* **Sadie** *by the wrist-*

The Woman   No-

Mrs Lyall   You will sit and perform your duty, Sadie-

The Woman   That's not my name-

Mrs Lyall   Then what shall I call you? Wretch? Traitor?
You deny me once more and I'll toss you into a hole far darker
than the one I found you in.
I'll make sure the light *never* finds you.

The Woman   I *am* the light!

Pause.

The Woman   I'll give you what you want.
I will bring death here.
I'll give it all to you.
I'll show you how much pain one soul can endure.

Beat.

Mrs Lyall *breaks one of* **The Woman's** *fingers. She howls in pain.*

Mrs Lyall   If you insist on behaving as a beast, I will treat
you as one-

She breaks another.

Mrs Lyall   How dare you speak to me this way-
You will be quiet and do as you are told, or I will clip your
wings further-

She wrenches **The Woman** *back to her feet-*

Mrs Lyall   You've wasted enough of my time.

Hold still-

The Woman *begins to glow.*

Mrs Lyall *steps back in surprise.*

Mrs Lyall   …No- No more of these vulgar displays-

The Woman *watches her fingers snap back into place.*

She turns her attention back to **Mrs Lyall**.

We hear heavy footsteps approaching.

The **Knight** *emerges from the shadows behind* **The Woman**.

Mrs Lyall   Oh- Oh my…

He draws his sword.

Mrs Lyall *falls to her knees.*

The Woman *stands over her.*

Mrs Lyall   Oh my…

The Woman *vomits a glowing lava into* **Mrs Lyall's** *mouth.*

She chokes and splutters in panic, clawing at her throat and face.

The Woman *and the* **Knight** *fade away into the black as it closes in-*

6.
343 AD.
Mrs Lyall *writhes on the ground, hacking and coughing.*

We hear **The Woman** *screaming- Somewhere far away, in terrible pain.*

Mrs Lyall *sits up with difficulty and looks around at the darkness.*

The Woman   *(Off.)* meam lucem demere conantur...!

We hear someone approaching.

Aulus *is here, lit by a nearby fire.*

There's a hole where his nose should be.

Aulus   phantasma...

He draws his sword-

Mrs Lyall   Oh- Oh no-

Black.

II:
Fisher King

1.
1348.
A dungeon.
Haster *(The Knight) stands holding a torch, the sole source of light.*
He stares into the dark, waiting.
We hear a shifting of chains.

The Woman *steps forward into the light.*
She wears a huge iron collar, strung with chains leading off in all directions.

She and **Haster** *consider each other.*

2.
By a small fire, **Haster** *chews on a hunk of salted meat.*
The Woman *watches.*

Pause.

The Woman   Where are we going?

Pause.

The Woman   You won't say?

Pause.

The Woman   You'll take me from a place and not say
where…

Pause.

The Woman   Is it far?

Pause.

The Woman   How many days will it take to get there?

Pause.

Haster   Many.

Pause.

The Woman   But how many, though?

Haster   There is no number.

Pause.

The Woman   …but if you were to guess a number.

Pause.

The Woman   If you were to pack enough meat for the journey, how many days meat would-

Haster   Do you feel pain.

The Woman   …Yes.

Haster   Then stop your tongue lest I cause you to feel some.

Pause.

Haster   I am taking you south.
…
To the King.

Pause.

The Woman   Why?

Haster   You are his property.

The Woman   I'm no one's property-

Haster   You are of this land. You are his to own.

The Woman   Are you his property, too?

Pause.

The Woman   What does he want with me?

Haster   It is not your concern.

The Woman   It is my concern- It's *me*. I am my concern.

Pause.

The Woman   I know who you are.

Pause.

The Woman   I heard your stories.
They use them to scare children.
…
'If you don't get to sleep, Lord Haster'll come and take your
heads off!'

She grins.

Pause.

The Woman   They tell stories of me, too.

Haster   I hold no belief in them.

The Woman   …Well I don't believe yours.

Haster *fixes her with a stare, then drinks from a bladder of water.*

The Woman   You're hard to talk to.

Haster   I have no desire to speak to you.

The Woman   Do you ever desire to speak to anyone?
…
Would you ever give greetings to a person?
Or say 'Goodbye!'
…
…No one spoke to me there, either.
Where you found me.
…
They were afraid of me.
They kept me in more chains than a- A beast would need.
…
They wouldn't even look at me when they brought my meals.
…
And they brought me meals on every day, though I never took
one bite.
Nor one sip of water.
Or wine.
…
Nor goats milk.
…
Nor mead.
…
Nor broth.
…
Nor the juice of-

Haster   *Stop naming fluids.*
…

Did I not tell you to shut your hole?
…
I am taking you south.
No words will change your course.
Until we reach-

The Woman *jumps up and flees into the woods.*

Haster   Wh- Hold- Woman!

Haster *struggles to his feet and after her-*

Haster   *Woman!*

He blunders wildly through the trees, changing directions repeatedly, soon lost.

He's moved too far from the fire, and the moonlight has deserted him.

We listen to his breathing, his faltering steps.

Haster   *Woman!*

Haster *walks on in total darkness.*

Eventually we hear someone approaching-

Len- *an ARP Warden- illuminates* **Haster** *with his hooded lantern.*

The two look at each other, dumbfounded.

An air raid siren begins to wail- **Haster** *backs away into the dark-*

Len   'Ere- You- Stop!

Haster *hurries away as the siren shifts in tone and length-*

A fluorescent strip light snaps into life above him-

He's in a tiled observation room.

The Woman *is here, ripping electrodes with long trailing wires from her body and skull. An alarm blares- A* **Figure** *in a fallout suit enters the room-*

Haster *stumbles away in fear as the light snaps off.*

He's running now, panicked-

Dim light far off in the distance casts strange shadows-

We can see figures hurrying about, we hear whispering- **The Woman's** *voice?*

Haster *draws his sword-*

Snatches of piano warp through the air.

We see a light coming near-

The Woman *steps into view.*

She is glowing.

3.
1993.
Ellen's *house.*
The Woman *stands caught under the hallway light.*

Ellen   Can I help you?

The Woman   ...

Ellen   Are you lost?

The Woman   …

Ellen   Hm?

The Woman   …I didn't think anyone lived here-

Ellen   So you just thought you'd come inside?

The Woman   The grass was long-

Ellen   Never you mind how long the grass is-
The grass being long doesn't mean you can just come into
someone's house.
…
I was planning on cutting it tomorrow if you must-
Never you mind how long it is.
Can you imagine what that feels like? Hearing someone
breaking into your home.

The Woman   The door wasn't locked-

Ellen   Do you do this a lot?
Waltz into people's houses? Help yourself?

The Woman   …Sometimes.

Ellen   You do?

The Woman   Only if they're not there.
I don't take anything.
I'm not a thief.

Ellen   So what are you then?

Pause.

Ellen   What's your name.

The Woman   …

Ellen   You don't have a name-?

The Woman   Brooke.

Ellen   Brooke.
Well, Brooke. Can you give me a reason why I shouldn't call the police?

Brooke   …

Ellen   Hm?

Brooke   …I-

4.
1348.
Woods.
The first light of dawn creeps through the trees.
Haster *tackles* **The Woman** *to the ground.*

The Woman   Let go- Let go of me-

Haster   Try and lose me with trickery?

The Woman   You followed me-

Haster   What was that- What was it?

The Woman   I can't control it- You said you don't believe-

Haster   *I do not!*

Pause.

Haster   I have no belief in magic, nor spirits, nor gods-
And I have no belief in *you.*
I believe only in *death*, and I will visit it upon you until it *sticks* if
you lead me astray again.

The Woman   I'm not afraid of you-

Haster   Nor I you, Girl.

5.
1979.
Evan's *Room.*
A tatty lamp shows us how dingy and cluttered it is.

Evan   Man I'm glad to see you. Like, I'm glad to see anyone,
you know? A *person.*
I haven't left this room in I don't even know- I heard you
knocking and I was like 'What's that?', Like I didn't recognise
the sound- Like I'd forgotten other people existed, you know? I
get so wrapped up in what I'm doing sometimes-

The Woman   I found your leaflet-

Evan   Newsletter, yeah, you said. I'm actually surprised there's
still some of those knocking around- Where'd you find it?

The Woman   In the library. In a book about- About ghosts.

Evan   Spiritualism man, yeah. Nice.
I actually don't do that anymore- Leave them in library books
like that.

I kept getting mentals coming here. They'd find them and think
I was sending them secret messages- Which in a way I was.
This guy showed up once without a shirt on talking about
satellites and then he got his cock out. Made me think I should
change my approach.
Also I kept getting in trouble with librarians.
You said you're researching-

The Woman   I have a degree.

Evan   You're- You're doing a degree?

The Woman   Yes. Yes.

Evan   Right. Well- You know- Be careful.
I got kicked out of uni for writing about this stuff.
Kicked out slash dropped out.

The Woman   Why?

Evan   Academics don't consider it history.

The Woman   What do they consider it.

Evan   Folklore. Myth. You know-
Shite, depending on who you ask.
But- And I've always said this-
You go back far enough and everything turns to myth. You
know?

The Woman   ...No.
...
You don't look like a historian.

Evan   Oh- Like- What's a historian meant to look like?

The Woman   Just- Different. To you.

Evan   Well I actually consider myself part of a new wave of
historians.
The old guard are all washed up-
They talk about the Tudors and Victorians the same way they
talk about the dinosaurs. Like they're dead.

The Woman   They are dead.

Evan   No, man. They're all still here. Like static.
We're wrapped *around* them.

6.
1993.
Brooke *and* **Ellen** *are watching TV.* **Ellen** *knits.*
She steals glances at **Brooke** *every now and then.*

Narrator *(TV.)*   -multiple skulls with head trauma suggesting
tribal conflict in the area.

Academic *(TV.)*   Several communities made homes here
due to the proximity of the river, with the nearby forestland
providing essential fuel and sustenance.

Narrator *(TV.)*   Simple flint tools suggest a rapidly developing
people determined to impose their will-

Ellen *turns the TV off.*

Pause.

Ellen   Did you wipe the tiles down afterwards?

Brooke   Yes.

Ellen   …Well you look better for a wash.

…

I can't get you to eat anything.

Brooke   No.

Ellen   Nothing to drink.

Brooke   *(Shakes head.)*

Pause.

Ellen   Is there somewhere I can drive you.
Do you have somewhere-

Brooke   I'm not from anywhere.

Ellen   Everyone's from somewhere.

Pause.

Ellen   You've a face on you for someone who's been let into a warm house on a cold night.

…

You don't like me, you've decided?

…

Or you don't like anyone.

…

Everyone's the same to you.

…

Suit yourself.
We'll have the television back on.
That's what people do when they run out of things to say to each other.

She turns the TV back on and goes back to knitting.

This time **Brooke** *is the one stealing glances.*

Academic *(TV)*   -these statuettes we found here seem to represent a matriarchal society built in the image of a goddess-

7.
1979.
Evan *is showing* **The Woman** *various books and papers.*

Evan   So this is like a pretty standard place to start. Your meat and two veg. Here's Henry Six, middle of the fifteenth century, back end of the hundred years war, no one can be fucked anymore, everyone just wants done with it- So he goes and marries Margaret of Anjou, who is French.
Here's a painting of the wedding- Nice spread and everything, all your lords and ladies here, and-

The Woman   There.

Evan   Wh- Yeah. That's ah- Yeah. Good eye.
She looks a bit different each time but you can always tell it's her.
How she's drawn, or stitched or whatever- Slightly apart from the rest, this sort of glow around her- Classic.
So for ages people were like, who *is* that, you know- So-

The Woman   I already know this.

Evan   Oh-

The Woman   Your leaflet-

Evan   Newsletter.

The Woman   It wasn't talking about this, it was saying how-

Evan   I'm just building a story here- Like an overview for you-
But I'll speed it up a bit if you're gonna-
Here-
This is from earlier- Edward Three.
Still got the glow around her, but this time she's kind of a
monster-
(Reading.) 'And chains of iron were shackled to the demon's
throat.
And the demon held no hunger. Nor thirst.
Nor did it ever know sleep'.

The Woman   This isn't what you said-

Evan   I'm just showing you how she's different every time.
Sometimes she's a demon or a witch or something, and
sometimes she's like a Mother Nature kind of thing- But really
she's always kind of the same-
Here she is in the King's procession-
Here she is at war-
Here she is as a kind of a fairy-
Here she is being cut to pieces-
Here she is being burnt at the stake-

The Woman   Where are the others?

Beat.

Evan   What?

The Woman   You said- You wrote about them-
You said there were women who never slept, women who-

Evan   Woman. Singular.

Pause.

The Woman   …There are no others.

Evan   No, like-
That's kind of the point of the book-

He holds out a battered old book.

Evan   *The* Woman.
The Woman in Time.

Pause.

The Woman *takes the book and looks at it.*

Evan   That's where all this comes from. What my newsletters
are about.
…I'm sorry if I phrased something weird or made you think-
Like if I confused you-
…
Are you alright?

A roll of thunder that only **The Woman** *can hear.*

8.
1348.
A hilltop. Rain.
Haster *strikes a fire into life whilst* **The Woman** *watches, her wrists
bound.*
The rain eases.

Catch *is stood nearby.*

Catch   Share your heat?

Haster   …Move on.

Catch   I've meat to offer.
…
You'll not let a man rest his bones?

Haster   I'll have your bones out you don't move away-

The Woman   Let him stay.
…
You don't own the hill.

Haster   …

Haster *settles at the fire, his back to* **Catch**.
Catch *sits and takes some meat from his pack.*

Catch   I'm grateful to you.
You're headed south?

The Woman   Yes.

Haster   You'll not tell our business.

The Woman   I'll tell *my* business to who I care to.

Haster   …

Catch   Your daughter's got fire in her.

The Woman   I'm not his daughter.

Catch   I saw your hands bound-

The Woman   So you think I'm his daughter?

Pause.

Catch   There's a lot of sickness down that way.
People dying in the street.
Might be wise to change your plan.

He spits.

The Woman   Have you seen it?

Catch   My share.
Black flesh. Rot. Stink.
It took the King's daughter.
No one safe from it.
…
Not even the great Lord Haster.

Pause.

Haster   You've mistaken me.

Catch   You know who your companion is?

Beat.

The Woman   Yes.

Catch   When I marked you I had to introduce myself.
I've known your stories since I was a boy, sir.

Pause.

Catch   Do you know any of them yourself?

Pause.

The Woman   The Village in the Hills.

Catch   That's a colourful one.
Not a tale you forget easy.
Innards strung through the trees like ribbon.
Men nailed by their tongues to their burning homes.
Speared heads lining the road like sentinels.
They said you could taste the blood on the air for miles around.

The Woman   …Is it true.

Catch   Oh, it's true. That and hundreds like it.
Back when he was the most feared knight living.
Before he lived long enough to become…*this*.
…
They say the King has tired of him now.
Won't have him near.
Truth is he's envious.
All a man wants is to become a story. To persist.
Our friend here's carved his name into history deeper than-

Haster   You've had your meeting.
Now fuck off.

Pause.

Catch *spits. He starts packing away his few things.*

Catch   I'd hoped you could help me.
I'm looking for someone.

The Woman   Who?

Catch   A woman.
Some strange kind of a woman is what they say.

Beat.

The Woman   …what do they say.

Catch   They say- She's lived longer than the mountains.
Longer than the rivers have run.
They say-
Doesn't matter which way you cut her.
How many pieces you put her into.
She'll come whole again and draw breath.
…
Talk is they found her in a village north of here.
Once her strangeness was known, they put her on a fire to burn.
They say she stepped down and walked free.
Never felt the flames.

The Woman   …I heard different.

Catch *spits.*

Catch   Course it's all shite.
Old stories for old cunts.
But some of these cunts have deep purses.
Deeper even than the King's, who wants her for himself.
Has some idea he can take the strangeness from her.
Make himself the same.

Pause.

Catch   It's shaming to see he sent his most feared knight
chasing a children's tale.
…
His *former* most feared knight-

Haster *draws his sword and turns-*
Catch *leaps on him and drives his knife into his side-*

Catch   That's all you can give me?

I've waited my whole life to kill you- This is how it is?

He clambers to his feet and spits.

Catch   Don't fear-
I'll tell them it was a fight for the ages.
That you were hate incarnate.
I want to kill the legend, not the old man behind it-

He turns to **The Woman***, who spits in his eye-*

Catch   Ah-
…
We've a long way to go together- You want to start like this?
You-
…

He rubs at his eye more frantically as it begins to burn-

He drops to the ground in pain, the scene around him fading.

9.
Lower Paleolithic Age.
We hear a rhythm being pounded on rock.

Catch *looks up from his writhing as a horn blows-*
We're in a cave, lit by flickering flames.

The Woman *steps into the light and stands before him-*
She wears a headdress of bones.

Catch   Oh God-
…
Oh God-

The **Man** *in hides from earlier approaches from behind with a sharpened stone-*

Catch   Oh God-

He pulls **Catch's** *head back to slash his throat-*

The Woman   No!

10.
1993.
A bedroom.
Light is flooding in from the hallway.

Ellen   What's the matter?

Pause.

Brooke   ...N-Nothing.

Ellen   You were shouting- Do you know what time it is?

Brooke   No-

Pause.

Ellen   You had a bad dream.

Brooke   I thought I was somewhere else.

Ellen   Well you're here. Fourteen Parklands Drive.
Nothing much going on here this time of night.
(Looking out the window.) ...We're the only light on, see?

Brooke   You can go back to bed- I'm sorry-

Ellen   It's alright. I'll stay a minute.
Get your bearings back.

Pause.

Ellen   You've raced through your library books again.

Brooke   Yes.

Ellen   You can come with me this time. Pick them out
yourself.

Brooke   No thank you.

Ellen   Well I never know what to get you.

Brooke   I don't mind.

Ellen   I don't know what someone your age- How old are
you?

Brooke   ...

Ellen   You really should leave the house at some point.

Brooke   You don't have to worry about me.

Ellen   Well I do. I don't have much choice in that anymore.
You won't eat anything. You won't go anywhere-
I don't think you sleep, either- I hear you talking to yourself-
Sadie if you will be difficult-

Brooke   You're not my mother.

Ellen   ...No. I'm not trying to be.

Pause.

Brooke   I'll leave if you want me to-

Ellen   That's not what I said, is it.

Pause.

Ellen   You know, I don't sleep much either.
Not for a long time.

Brooke   …Since your son died.

Pause.

Ellen   …How do you know about that.

Brooke   You have pictures. But you don't talk about him.

Ellen   …Well.
Yes.
…

Brooke   That's why you let me stay here.

Pause.

Ellen   I'm letting you stay because you don't have anywhere
else to go.

Brooke   You want-

Ellen   I don't want anything from you, Brooke.
Other than to get some fresh air every now and then.
…
You know you can stay as long as you like.

…

Plenty of space here, someone might as well make use of it.

Pause.

Ellen   Do you have them a lot. These dreams.
Or whatever they are.

Brooke   *(Nods.)*

Ellen   Bad things. That happened to you. Or-

Brooke   People find me. When it's dark.

Ellen   *(Nods.)* …What was this one.
You say it out loud, it'll fritter away to nothing.

Pause.

Brooke   …I was in a box.
Underwater.
They put me in a box underwater.

Ellen   Who did?

Brooke   A- Soldier.
…
I was in there a long time.
I was drowning. Over and over again.

Ellen   Did you get out?

Brooke   There was a sword somehow-
…
I used it to break the wood- It was rotten.
I swam to the surface.

…
There was a man there. Young.
He was good to me.
Until he wasn't.
Until I wasn't any use to him anymore.

Pause.

Brooke   You wouldn't want me here if you knew what I was.

Ellen   And what's that.

Brooke   …I'm different from everyone else.

Ellen   I'll tell you a secret-
Everyone's different from everyone else.
You seem very sure how I feel about things.
You should ask me, next time.
…
You tell your own story.
And don't let others tell it for you.

11.
1979.
The Woman *is looking through the book.*

Evan   'for she dwells
Down in a deep; Calm, whatsoever storms
May shake the world'.
That's Tennyson.
…
There she is giving Arthur his special sword and everything.

The Woman   …Excalibur.

Evan   There you go. That's who started all this anyway.

The Woman *closes the book and looks at the cover.*

The Woman   Dorothy Waites.

Evan   She's the one connected all the paintings and accounts and everything.
Tapestries. Statues.
Traced her all the way back to folk tales.

The Woman   Does she still-

Evan   *(Shakes head.)* Dead. Ages ago.
That was the last thing she wrote. And they didn't print many copies, so if you could be careful with it-

The Woman   Can I keep it?

Evan   Wh- No- Not-

He takes it back.

Evan   Sorry, but-
This is like my most- Irreplaceable, you know?
…You can come back and look at it.
Whenever you like.
Or you can wait and read my book.
My book about the book. That's what I'm doing now, see, so-

The Woman   How does it end.

Evan   …How does it-

The Woman   What does it say happens to her.

Beat.

Evan   She's not real, man. There's no eternal…
She's a symbol. Like a wooden horse. Prometheus.
She's just something people were painting into history as this
kind of indicator.
Like how she's depicted tells us the mood of the time. Or the
King's standing or whatever. Like a mascot.
…
It's a kind of a game that's been running for centuries. That's
what the book proved.
Argued, I should say.

The Woman *nods.*

The Woman   …a game.

Pause.

Evan   I get how you feel-
You know.
…
I spend so much time with her sometimes *I* forget.
One of my lecturers- Before I left-
He said I talked like I was in love with her.
Like I'd fallen in love with this painting. This idea.
And sometimes it does feel-
When I'm looking for her, now?
I try and find her in contemporary- You know.
It feels like I'm hunting a missing person sometimes.
Someone lost.
…
And I feel bad no one ever gave her a name.
That's something we all get given, right?

12.
1348.
The hilltop.
Haster *wakes with a start. The fire has burnt down to embers.*

The Woman   ...You're still breathing.
...
You were shouting at someone. In your sleep.

Pause.

Haster *struggles to sit up, clutching his wound.*
He looks around suddenly-

The Woman   I sent him away.

Haster   ...Where.

The Woman   Away.

Beat.

Haster   You said you had no control-

The Woman   I don't. Mostly.

Haster   ...But you've done the same to others.

The Woman   When I was able.
Sometimes I had to.
I'm not like you.

Pause.

Haster   Why stay.
Why wait for me to wake-

The Woman   He wants to steal my light.

Haster   …

The Woman   How does he hope to do it.
Some way that hurts me.

Haster   …I know not what-

The Woman   But you'll take me to him anyway.
Whatever he might do to me-

Haster   He is my king.
I go where I am told.

The Woman   And kill who you are told.
…
No one can take it from me.
Many have tried.

Pause.

The Woman *moves over to him.*
She pushes a finger into his wound.
Haster *grunts and struggles.*

The Woman   You've lost a lot of yourself.
Are you afraid?

Haster   …

The Woman   You sounded as if you were.
…
What did you see? That made you cry out.

Pause.

Haster   My first kill.

The Woman   Who was it.

Pause.

Haster   A boy.
A boy I knew.
…
I was alone as a child.
Without name.
Slept in the woods.
Others chased me for sport.
Beat me.
…
I took a rock.
Put an end to the leader of their pack.

The Woman   …He finds you at night.

Haster   They all do.

Pause.

The Woman   Where did you find your name.

Haster   The King. He named me.

The Woman   He's like your father.

Haster   I am a monster to him.
He cannot meet my eye.
…
A man doesn't let his dog eat at the table.

The Woman   People call me monster, too.

Haster   They also call you God.

The Woman   I don't want to be a god.

Haster   Better that than monster.

The Woman   I want to be like everyone else.

Haster   What hope is there of that.
…
For either of us.

The Woman   The village I was at before.
They let me stay.
I liked feeding the horses.
Caring for the children.
They taught me to dance.

Haster   And when they discovered you?

The Woman   …

Haster   Plenty are willing to be near me as well. Until they learn my name.
…
Better to have no name.
To be forgotten.

The Woman   Once I forgot who I was.
I gave up and hid myself away until it all left me.
And I had peace.
But in time it came back to me.
At first I'd hear my own stories and think there were others like how I was.
Then I'd come to realise.
And all of it would return.

And that was worse than any pain before.
Any pain you could ever make a person feel.

Haster   …You have what men have wanted as long as they
have lived-

The Woman   I have *nothing*.
…
I am denied myself by others telling me what I am.
What purpose I serve to them.
I have seen more than anyone alive, but know less of myself
than a child.

Haster   Through living you must have some knowledge of-

The Woman   Why? You men have walked almost as long as
I, and you haven't learned anything.
…
I have no knowing even-
If I ever come to an end.
…
Do any of the stories tell of that?
Or am I denied that too.

Pause.

Haster *is losing more and more blood.*

The Woman *moves closer to him.*

She takes his knife.

A moment.

She cuts her thumb open.

The Woman   Hold on to me.

...

Hold *on* to me.

Haster *takes her wrist.*

She presses her thumb into his wound- It glows.

Haster *roars in pain-*

13.
1994.
Haster *is bleeding out on* **Ellen's** *floor, still clutching* **Brooke's** *wrist.*
A sitcom burbles away on the TV.
Ellen *stands in the doorway holding a mug.*

Pause.

Brooke   Help.

Ellen   ...wh- How-

Brooke   I had to bring him here.

Ellen   From- Where- He's bleeding-

Brooke   He needs h/elp-

Ellen   Who is he? How did you get him here? I leave the room for a second-

Brooke   He's hurt-

Ellen   That's not answering-

Brooke   You're a nurse.

Ellen   *Retired.* I'm a retired nurse- And that doesn't mean you can bring bleeding men in off the-

Brooke   He's my friend.
…
I need you to help me.

Pause.

Ellen *steps closer and peers at* **Haster**.

Ellen   What's happened to him?

Brooke   Someone attacked him- A knife-

Ellen   He needs to go to hospital-

Brooke   He can't-

Ellen   Why not?

Brooke   It won't make sense to you.

Ellen   It doesn't- None of this-

Brooke   We can't go to hospital.
Please.

Beat.

Ellen *leaves.*

Brooke   Ellen-!

Ellen   *(From off.)* I'm coming back- Hold your horses-

She reappears with a tool box stuffed with medical supplies, kneeling down next to **Haster**.

Ellen   Shift. Let me see-
…
Press very hard, there.
He's lucky.

She starts unpacking her supplies; cleaning the wound.

Ellen   Most of this stuff is out of date…

Brooke   It doesn't matter.

Ellen   …Why is he dressed like this? He got attacked in fancy dress?

Haster *is trying to let go of* **Brooke**-

Brooke   Hoo- Holde to me. She helpe thee, fool.

Ellen   …Hold this. Here. He needs stitches.

Brooke   So you can-

Ellen   I'm not stitching a knight closed on my living room floor- I don't have-

Brooke   Then he'll die.

Ellen   …
(To **Haster**.*)* This will hurt.
Is he listening to me?

Haster *has turned his head to watch the sitcom on TV, incredulous.*

Brooke   He's fine. Do it.
…I mean- Please.

Ellen *begins stitching him closed.*

Ellen   …How do you make a friend like this?
How are you making *any* friends. You barely leave the house.

Brooke   He's from a long time ago.

Ellen   I'll say. He smells.

Brooke   He helped me.

Ellen   How's that.

Brooke   He took me somewhere safe.
…
We helped each other.

Ellen   …How did you get him in here so quickly.

Brooke   I told you-

Ellen   You did not.

Brooke   I told you I'm not like anyone else.

Ellen   …Clearly.

She cleans the site of the wound and dresses it.

Ellen   That's the best I can do, but I can't-

Brooke   She mended thee.

Haster   What thyng is this-

Brooke   It kepe thee heeld, leve it. I sende thee agayn now.

Haster   /No-

Ellen   What are you talking like that f-

The Woman *pulls* **Haster's** *hand from her wrist-*

14.
1348.
They're back on the hilltop, the embers still glowing.
Haster *stands shakily and looks around.*

Pause.

Haster   What was that place.

The Woman   …

Haster   You took me-

The Woman   I don't know where.
…
I told you. I don't have control.

Haster   But you know-

The Woman   I can only see- Pieces of it.

Haster   …

Haster *feels at his side-*
Lifts his shirt to reveal the dressing.

The Woman   What is it?

Haster   ...I am mended.

Pause.

The Woman   I won't go south with you.
...
I won't be taken anywhere I don't choose myself.
Anywhere I am to be hurt- I won't let you-

Haster   North.
...
We'll go north.
...Should you choose.
...
You'll be safer across the border.

Pause.

The Woman   You'll go with me.

Haster   ...*(Nods.)*
I will get you there. Without harm from others.

The Woman   You hate me.

Haster   ...I have tried hating you.
I am unable.

Pause.

She stands.

The Woman   North-

Haster   I am in your debt-

The Woman   Then you can be kind to me.
You can talk to me about whatever I choose, all the way to
wherever it is-

Haster   I will give you a gift.
…
Should you choose to keep it.

Pause.

Haster   Brooke.
…
It means-
River.
…
It is true to what you are.

15.
1353.
*A forest, somewhere in the Highlands. Shafts of sunlight pierce the canopy
above.*

Mason *is here, his face a bloodied wreck.*
He looks around, terrified.

Pause.

He hears something and turns-

Brooke *emerges from the trees, her longbow poised.*

Brooke   What are you doing here?

Mason   ...

Brooke   This is our place, no one's to come here.

Mason   I- I-

We hear **Haster** *before he appears, carrying firewood-*

Haster   You'll have me do all the labour? Cook your meals, build your fires-

He sees **Mason** *and draws a knife-*

Haster   Step back.
Back.

Mason *staggers and falls back, scrambling to his feet.*

Haster   This is our land-

Brooke   I told him.

Haster   What brings you here?

Brooke   I asked him.

Haster   And what did he tell you.

Mason   I- I- I-

Brooke   This. Where's your sword?

Haster   You know well it is lost- Likely by you-

Brooke   I didn't lose it- You should be more careful with it-

Mason *points to* **Brooke**-

Haster   You'll put that down should you want to keep it.

Mason *drops his arm.*
Brooke *has wandered closer.*

Brooke   His clothes are strange.

Haster   Step away.

Brooke   He's hurt-

Haster   Step *away*.
…
Brooke.

Brooke   He's scared-

Haster   As he should be.
(To **Mason**.*)* Down on your knees.

Mason *drops to his knees.*

Brooke   No-

Haster   I'll make it quick.

Brooke   He's lost, he didn't do anything-

Haster   You don't know what he's doing here- He will lead others to us.
Move-

Brooke   No.

Haster   You want to be found?

Brooke   I won't let you kill people without cause-

Mason *starts singing in a high, manic yell-*

> Only a thin veil between us,
> My loved ones so precious and true-
> Only as mist before sunrise,
> I am hidden away from your view-

Beat.

Haster   What is this-

Again, louder-

> Often I come with your blessing,
> And strive all your sorrows to share-

Brooke *yanks* **Haster's** *arm behind his back-*

Brooke   Run! Run!

Mason *trips and stumbles away.*

After a moment, she releases **Haster**.

Haster   Now I'm to hunt him-

Brooke   You'll not catch him. Not with your knees.
…
Old man.

Haster   …

Brooke   Let's go home. It's time to eat.

Haster   You'll see how wise a decision you made when he returns-

16.
1999.
Brooke *stands in the hall of Ellen's now-dingy house.*
Sunlight floods in from outside, around the shape of **Alice**.

Alice   You didn't hear me knocking? Shouting through the letterbox?
I could see you moving around in here. Why didn't you answer?

Brooke   I-

Alice   Are you Ellen Harpley? No- You look too young-

Brooke   I just live here.

Alice   With Miss Harpley?

Brooke   Yes.

Alice   So where is she?

Brooke   …

Alice   I'll need to speak with her if I'm to-

Brooke   She's gone.

Beat.

Alice   Gone. Gone how. Where.

Brooke   She's-

Alice   Dead?

Brooke   ...(*Nods.*)

Pause.

Alice   You do know when someone dies you need to tell people.
People need to know.
I'm here as part of a possession action, do you know what that is?

Brooke   N-

Alice   It means the bank is taking back this house.
It means a lot of money is owed.
Isn't the power off? The gas? You didn't think to ask why?
...
Was it like this when she was here?
The windows blocked off- All these books-

Brooke   I don't have answers to any of your questions.

Alice   Well if you want to prove you have a claim to the house
you'll need to find some. For all I know you could be-
Are you a relative? Friend?
How did you come to be living here?
When did she die?

Brooke (*Backing away.*)   I'll just leave- I can leave-

Alice   No, wait a minute- Hold on- Stop-
Who are you?

Brooke   No one- I'm no one-

17.
1360.
Brooke *clambers up into the mouth of a cave.*
She looks down into it- The late sun is only creeping down the first few feet.

Haster *comes into view, struggling.*
Brooke *tries to help him, but he waves her away.*
He throws his stick up into the cave and drags himself up the rest of the way.

Brooke   This is it?

Retrieving his stick and standing, **Haster** *tosses a rock down into the cave.*
They listen to it bounce down.

Haster   It's deep.
Go and see.

Brooke   …This is what you made us walk here for?

Haster   Hm.

Brooke   You dragged yourself this whole way to show me a cave?
You won't even walk with me round the lake anymore.

Pause.

Brooke   Well. You've shown me.
Let's go-

Haster   No.
…

Go down and look-

Brooke   At what? It's getting dark, we have to head back-

Haster   We're not going back.

Pause.

Haster   You'll live here now.
…
Go down as deep as you can.
Stay hidden.

Pause.

Brooke   No-

Haster   I'm old. No time left.
You'll stay here.
Wait until this plague or the next finishes them all.
…
Once every man woman and child has rotted away to naught,
You can come out.
You'll be safe.

Brooke   I won't-

Haster   I can't protect you-

Brooke   I don't need your protection-

Haster   They will find you.

Brooke   Who?

Haster   *Any*one.

…
Any of them.

Pause.

Brooke   I won't stay here.

Haster   You will.

Brooke   I'm going home. To *our* home.
The home we built together.
People don't live in caves-

Haster   Well you are not people.
…
Are you.

Pause.

Haster   Did you expect this would last forever?
This playing at being a family?
Serving you your imagined meals each night.
Did you not see time cutting at me?
…
I have done you more harm than any of them-

Brooke   You gave me my name-

Haster   And what good will it serve you?
What good is pretending you're something other than what you
are?

Pause.

Brooke   Where will you go?

Haster   …While I've my strength-
Tear the hut down-

Brooke   Our *home*-

Haster   Walk into the lake.

Pause.

Haster   You will forget me.

Brooke   I won't.

Haster   In time you will.

Brooke   Never.
…
Even if everything else is stolen from me, I'll remember you.
Always.
I'll chain you to my thoughts and drag you through time.
…
And I will never stay here.
I'll find others-
I'll find others to be with-

Haster   And they will hate you. Over and again.
Or else die and leave you, just as I do now.
Let me leave knowing you will spare yourself the pain.

Brooke   I won't be your redemption.
You're the same as the rest- Wanting me to heal you-

Haster   There is no healing me.

Brooke   As soon as you're gone, I'll leave.

Haster   You'll find sense.

Brooke   I'll *run*.
I'll run as fast as I can-

Haster   Then *go*.
Go back to be burnt.
Drowned.
To be cleaved open and peered at.
There is no home for you.
There can never be.

Brooke   You're my home-

Haster   I wish I'd never laid eyes on you.

Brooke   That's not true-

Haster   You have brought me nothing but confusion-
I ought to hack you to pieces and throw you down there-
Seal it up.

Brooke   I love you-

Haster *advances on her darkly-*

Haster   Don't ever say that.
…
To anyone.
…
I am *death*.
I have killed more than any could number.
I am monstrous-

The Woman   You are *nothing.*

The Woman *glows with a furious rage, terrifying-*
Haster *falls backwards, retreating-*

The Woman   A *smear* of flesh.
I am *all*.
Your armies are *ants* before me.
I will show you what death is-
I will lay waste to *everything*.
I will raze this earth with a fire undying-
I will splinter every soul into pieces, to scatter through time in unending pain.
I will be everything they say I am and more-
And I'll make you watch.
I will leave nothing but the two of us and *dust*.

She calms, her light fading.

The Woman   ...I'll show you how I hate them.
How I'm just like you.

Pause.

Haster   We both know you are not.

Pause.

Haster *struggles to his feet.*

The Woman   I won't stay here.

Haster   ...Then you'll come back.
...
The youth in your voice will sour,
and you'll come back.
...
...

Goodbye, Woman.

Haster *leaves.*

18.
1998.
Brooke *and* **Ellen** *are walking on the beach together.*
The low afternoon sun shimmers on the waves as they wash onto the sand.

Ellen   He used to make me bring him here every weekend.
One Christmas he asked for a metal detector, so then every
Sunday we'd be here looking for treasure.
Never found much, of course.
I think his best find was someone's keys they'd dropped walking
the dog.
They gave him a fiver as reward.
I think we spotted those without the detector, to be honest.
…
We met a few others doing it once- Older.
He thought they'd want to talk about Roman coins and the
like, but they were mostly just interested in finding bits of lost
jewellery to sell.
People can be disappointing sometimes.

Ellen *has stopped-*

Ellen   …What was I talking about?
…
My head's a sieve these days, I can't even-

Brooke   Coming here. Looking for treasure.

Beat.

Ellen   Oh.

…
Yes.
…
…
Now he's under the ground himself.

Pause.

Brooke   What did that feel like?

Pause.

Ellen   It was very-
Unusual.
That's a daft thing to-
…
I couldn't imagine it.
What he'd felt-
It was strange. Trying to think about something I couldn't
imagine.
…
I stopped sleeping.
I'd watch the sun come up every morning and think-
'There's been a mistake'. You know-
'The sun can't keep coming up when this has happened'.
'Someone should tell someone'.
How strange.
…
I really didn't do anything much for a very long time.

Pause.

Brooke   How did you keep going?

Ellen   …Well. You just do, don't you.
…

I didn't want to live my life as one long dying.
I started to try my best to think differently about things.
It took a bit of time, but eventually-
I'd think-
That-
The joy of knowing him was greater than the pain of losing him.
That I was lucky, in some ways.
That I'd had someone to feel sad to lose.
Lots of people don't have that.
…

I'd think how the past is still here in all sorts of ways.
It's not gone, really- It's just-
Taken a different shape.
…

I'd think-
There's always chance-
For something new.

Pause.

Ellen   Look at us-!
Who'd have thought I'd meet you?
Who'd have thought you'd ever leave the house?

Pause.

Ellen   Come on, let's go home-

Brooke *kisses her.*

Beat.

Ellen   What was that for?
What's got into you?
…What's-

The sound of the waves has stopped.

Brooke *walks across to* **Evan**-

We're in his flat in **1979**.
Evan *is rolling a joint whilst* **The Woman** *reads the book.*

Ellen *stares at her son, awestruck.*

Evan Like I said man, studying this stuff doesn't get you fame
and glory- It gets you a damp room with a sink to piss in. Not
that fame and glory is why we're historians of course, but- Like-
A *bit* of glory would be nice. It's mostly a pretty thankless task.
Case in point- I found this one book written by a guy who was
an air raid warden- Self-published, you know- And in it, he
tells this story where he finds a woman in a bomb site with two
broken legs. In pain, obviously.
But when he goes to help her, her legs just- Click! Snap back
into place, and she runs off. So I thought, nice, someone
keeping the torch burning, another enthusiast.
So I track the guy down to a care home and he tries to convince
me it's *true*- Says he's never read the Waites book. Says no one
ever believed him, but he knows what he saw- And on top
of *that* he starts telling me he saw a ghost as well, a knight in
armour wandering about-
And I was trying to be polite and all, but I guess he'd gone
senile, or-
…What?

Evan *notices* **The Woman** *staring at* **Ellen**, *stood behind him.*

Pause.

He turns to see what she's looking at-

The scene vanishes.

The Woman *is left alone.*

19.

The Woman   Alone,
I waited.

Whilst land and water were at war, I watched-
As mountains swept the earth in rolling tides,
The ground beneath my feet a churning mire.

And I walked alone.
And waited.

Through an age of smoke and fog.
Through the supremacy of plants.
Through crowds of beasts indifferent to me,
Who dragged themselves ashore to claim what life
They could before the rains of fire and stone
Cut short their time and drove them into dust.

Until at last I found-
I saw-
Emerging from the trees-
Their spines straightening-
Eyes lifting...
...Here.

I watched them learn.
And love.
And take delight in their young.
And dance...
I watched them choose to move themselves in rhythm with their
hearts.
With the hearts of others-
Beating.
On and on.
As they pushed their breath onto the embers of a new era-

And marked me separate from themselves.

Set me apart.

Crowned me some exalted other as they
Clothed me in the tales they told, to thrust me
In a role I'd never sought to play, and
Split themselves along imagined lines to
Spill their blood as though their streams were endless,

And oftentimes I'd grow so tired I'd make
Myself forget. I'd hide myself away
And close my eyes in pantomime of sleep,
Waiting. As time stole all I knew from me.
But back each happening came against my will,
Fast rising in my throat like jagged stones,
To tell me once again I am alone.

And so I broke.

And returned. To a place from long ago-
A cave. Once claimed for me by one I'd known-
A friend.

And I descend, in hope I'd find some trace
Of him remained, to sit hidden from light,
And let the insects make their homes within my flesh-
And feel my skin fuse fast into the rock,
And wish with everything to fall asleep.

And I become a children's tale, a myth.

A footnote in books left unread on shelves.

Until the time they make me real again.
And bring themselves outside my cave to beg.

To keen. To plead deliverance. To pray.

I hear their sorrow drifting down but tell
Myself it's all a dream, a cruel nightmare,
The issue of a weary broken heart.
So conjure up another in its place-
A woman born who lived without event,
And died surrounded by her family,
Stitched tight with all through her impermanence.

And then they're gone.

And I emerge, beneath skies of puce and rust,
To walk across a sea of bones bleached white
As what few living things remain come circling,
Seeking comfort as their faltering hearts
Slow gently to a halt. I sit and watch
The withered trees and plants retreating fast,
The final structures tumbling into ash,
Then climb upon the tallest peak to see
The sun colossal, drawing nearer still,
Seducing stone to ecstasies of fracture
As everything below diminishes
Through immolation, losing shape and sense
As gases flare and burst up through the ground
In colours never visible before-
The bacchanal above in harmony,
A boiling tumult hurling tendrils out
To wrap my form and coax my feet to leave
The roiling earth below and form the new
Axis amongst the stars, as from beyond
Race planets, orbits snapped, colliding with
Their many-numbered moons with thunderous force-
The stars in their quintillions closing in
To veil my shape with bloated swelling forms,
Then bursting in totality, now come

Annihilating orchestras of light-

Until as quick the all shrinks to a point
Of brilliance infinitesimal-

Drifting about the void we're held within.

I reach, and let it sail into my hands.
And know this spark might come to life anew-
Should I choose to ignite it with a breath.

This light and I. Alone. Together.

And I think of her.

And what she told me.

And I cradle the glow.
And wait.
And wonder.

Appendix

All other characters are to be played by the performers playing
Mrs Lyall, Mason, and Haster.

Here is the suggested breakdown:
Mrs Lyall – Ellen; Alice
Mason – Aulus; Len; Evan; Catch
Haster – Man (I:5/II:9).

Figure (II:2), Narrator and Academic can be assigned to any of
the three.

*

The song that commences the séance is 'Only a Thin Veil
Between Us' by C. Payson Longley. It was written after 1863,
but I think you can give me a break.
I am thankful to Matt Marble and his music preservation
website Secret Sound Project (mattmarble.net/secret-sound)
for providing me with the sheet music.

*

Thanks to Rory Mullarkey for his translations and support
throughout the writing.

I am grateful to the books *The Darkened Room* by Alex Owen
and *The Table Rappers* by Ronald Pearsall for guiding me
through the world of Victorian spiritualism; and of course
The Woman in Time by Dorothy Waites for providing much of
the play's central conceit.

The work of Jessie Weston and Margaret Murray has long been beloved by those who crawl literature's cobweb of intertextuality. *From Ritual to Romance* (1920) and *The Witch-Cult in Western Europe* (1921) both took their cues from Charles Frazer's *The Golden Bough* (1890-1915), applying aspects of that work's thesis to Grail literature and the study of western witchcraft respectively. Though both books have now been fairly definitively debunked, through their ambition and imagination, they have attained a form of immortality in certain circles.

Within these circles, it's not uncommon to hear another name spoken; that of Dorothy Waites and her book *The Woman in Time* (1928). Like her contemporaries, Waites was inspired by Frazer's grand work to write her own study of myth and folklore. But whilst Weston and Murray's books have enjoyed frequent rediscovery by new generations of readers, *The Woman in Time* has remained obscure, largely unread by the general public.

The Woman in Time was Waites' only book, following a handful of solid if unremarkable papers published in small press history journals. From what little we can piece together of her biography, we know she was a 'scholar' rather than a formally qualified historian or theorist, and seemed to have fallen into writing after a lifetime spent in libraries. It seems likely she was something of a recluse. *The Woman in Time* is one of the last traces left of Waites, and with so few copies existing, that too is on the brink of vanishing. Published only a few months prior to her death, the print run was so small that the book barely registered on publication.

+

The book's thesis is (in somewhat rudimentary terms) articulated within the play here: Waites gathered as many accounts and paintings as she could find of nameless, mysterious women in high places, and attributed them all to a single, fictional personage: 'The Woman' of the title. She argued this woman was a symbol used to pass comment on the age, a kind of social thermometer; a monumental inside joke that has somehow lasted for the entirety of recorded history in this country.

It's a charming thesis in many ways, a secret chain wrought by artists and historians, 'The Woman' being something of a baton pass between the ages. The ears of anyone with a love for history would prick up at the idea of such a wheeze.

But as charming as the concept may be, it's plainly nonsense. Putting aside the basic administrative difficulties of sustaining such a thing, let's consider what little 'evidence' Waites gives us in support of her theory.

+

Firstly, the sheer numbers of these appearances in paintings are remarked upon. Time after time Waites finds a forlorn figure in amongst scenes of weddings, coronations, battles; all sharing a superficial resemblance.
This is easy enough to dismiss. Of course there are many unidentified women in the paintings she highlights; half the people in *all* paintings from across time we have next to no information on, *especially* the women. The resemblance is down to a hefty dose of confirmation bias.

There's also the question of what need there would be for such a symbol. Practically *everything* in a portrait of a royal, or dignitary, or religious figure from the earliest time to now is a symbol of some kind. The choice of colour, the quality of light,

the presence of animals, or children, or angels: I could go on
and on. It's all but impossible for an artist to paint someone and
not reveal their opinion of that person. It's not an original idea
that portraits are more often a painting of the artist rather than
the subject.

The second half of *The Woman in Time* is given over to the
various scraps of writing Waites has decided are also part
of this scheme. Mostly letters and diary entries, with a few
other accounts and poems thrown in. These are what the
'true believers' of the book (who we'll come to in due course)
base their skewed world view on, and it's true that some are
bizarre enough to raise an eyebrow; but just as it's true I have
no definitive explanation for some of these accounts, I also
have no definitive explanation for a whole host of peculiarities
throughout historical record. If we had answers for everything,
there would be no further need for historians. But in an effort
to provide the titillation Mr McDowell was no doubt hoping for
when he commissioned this essay, I'll paste a selection of *The
Woman*'s 'greatest hits' here:

Letter from an unknown sender, presumed circa 1216:
  'I fear your downfall if you do not keep closer watch on the
  woman than you have been.
  Often I hear of an attempt to steal her away, by men
  presumed faithful to you.
  It is known you do not hold the woman in as high regard as
  others, but be sure that the king will visit harm on you should
  she be lost to him whilst under your eye.'

Entry from The Diary of Samuel Pepys, 10th September 1665:
  'To Captain Cocke's, where I find my Lord Bruncker and his
  mistress, and Mr Rodley.
  Where we supped (there was also Sir W. Doyly and Mr.
  Evelyn); Mr Rodley regaled us once more with his encounter
  with the street girl who illuminated. His assurances of truth

did make us all die almost of laughing, and Lord Bruncker
did find new barbs to fire at the displeased Mr Rodley, which
was the very crown of our mirth.'

Letter from Professor F.R. Bailey to his brother, 1898:
'Further rumours of Her Majesty's affiliation with Mr Lees;
he has managed to extend his right of access to the palace
with the discovery of a peculiar girl of whom he has now
taken possession; said to exhibit the supposed qualities of an
ancient soul housed within a young body.
For how long this charlatan will continue to sustain interest in
his endeavours is for any to guess.
The foundations he builds his beliefs upon seem as ever-
shifting as sand.
Reincarnation now, of all things.'

When we collect a few of these accounts in one place, they take
on an undeniable air of intrigue; but in isolation they seem little
more than half-told, second-hand accounts of women of whom
we have no supporting information, and so those inclined can
fill in the gaps with fantasy.

And what gaps they are! I hardly need to point out the long
stretches of time between these accounts alone, and it's not as
if this supposed chain is unbroken for any length of time; it's a
fractured, hodgepodge collection that serves only to support the
imagined narrative.

+

It's key to remember that even the qualities of this woman were
decided by Waites herself; very few are to be found consistently
in the accounts she cites. She found a handful of women in
paintings surrounded by a glowing light, and so 'The Woman'
has 'an unearthly glow'. Of course, a woman surrounded by a
heavenly glow in a painting is hardly anything to write home

about: in the seventeenth century you'd be hard-pressed to find a woman in a painting who *wasn't* glowing.

To take the Pepys quote above as an example, there is no shortage of writing about strange light, or spontaneous combustion and the like, from the same period. Pepys himself was a fan of ghost stories, and in this entry he *himself* is laughing at the idea of a glowing woman hiding somewhere in London.

I have neither the space here nor the heart to continue dissecting the book, and it pains me somewhat to do what little I have here. Despite appearances I have a certain amount of respect and affection for Waites and her book: her passion for her subject is palpable, and it would have been no small feat to have a book like this published as an outsider in the academic community. But ultimately *The Woman in Time* is little more than a curio; a fantasy dreamt up by a lonely reader.

I once met a writer who attempted to convince me it was, in fact, an experimental novel; that Waites had written a postmodern text during the age of modernism. I am yet to be won over by this argument.

+

When published, the book was greeted with what we shall call a mixed response: most critics didn't respond to the book at all, perhaps not being aware of it; but the few that did were merciless. In *From Ritual to Romance*, Weston's tendency to only support a certain share of her claims with evidence had been a vulnerability her critics had attacked. She allowed her imagination to forge the remaining connections and move quickly on. Whilst both Weston and Murray's books contained more than a handful of these moments, *The Woman in Time* is practically defined by them. Waites' theory was more outlandish even than Murray's witch-cult, and presented even scanter evidence with which to support it. With hindsight, the irritating epigraph Weston used for *Ritual* warned us what was to come with Waites:

'Many literary critics seem to think that an hypothesis about obscure and remote questions of history can be refuted by a simple demand for the production of more evidence than in fact exists. - But the true test of an hypothesis, if it cannot be shewn to conflict with known truths, is the number of facts that it correlates, and explains.'

Origins of Attic Comedy
Francis MacDonald Cornford

The few words that were written about the book upon publication were openly hostile:

'Miss Waites has plainly taken leave of her senses'
British Mythology and Folklore: A Quarterly Review (Volume XXXIX)
H.L. Gooding

'Miss Waites cannot be of sound mind if she believes…any of us will swallow these ludicrous notions'
The Arthurian Literature Journal (August 1928)
William Henslow

Whilst in the main body of these reviews we detect the tone men reserve for deriding the intellectual pursuits of women, one can't counter the argument that with *The Woman in Time*, Dorothy Waites departed far from history and wrote a fairy tale.

With such a small print run the book quickly became a collector's item, and remains a rare volume to this day, usually only found within university libraries. An internet search throws up very few accessible copies, nor much in the way of extracts or digitised copies. It has survived thanks to the efforts of two very different groups: book collectors, and the small but intense group of misguided individuals that maintain 'The Woman' is a real person.

+

When I found an unkempt but polite young man outside my office one day waiting to ask me questions about Dorothy Waites, I was immediately on guard. Having had a few unpleasant run-ins with followers of 'The Woman', I wasn't best pleased to find one at my door. Practically my first words to Mr McDowell were 'You don't believe there really *is* an immortal woman tied to our shores, do you?'. I suppose it is rather revealing about the times in which we live that one can ask such a thing in all seriousness.

Five years ago, to my eternal regret, I published a paper that made mention of Waites' book. This resulted in my email inbox and university pigeon-hole being regularly filled with correspondence from all manner of − to put it kindly − eccentrics, eager to tell me about whichever new piece of 'evidence' had come to light that week. This is how I became aware of the book's current fanbase.

Whilst the majority of these people are harmless enough, there is a vocal minority who now dedicate much of their time to tell me in as many colourful ways as possible that I am 'suppressing the truth' or 'destroying' Waites' legacy. All of which hopefully goes some way to explain my reluctance to write any more on the subject.

+

Despite the various leaps of imagination Waites makes in her book, she never for a moment attempts to argue that 'The Woman' is a real person; an immortal cursed to watch all of this country's history pass before her. Her subject is symbols. How they are formed, used, and passed on down through the ages.

The first letter I received I assumed to be from one of my
colleagues, playing yet another juvenile practical joke on me.
But after a second arrived, I realised with horror that there were
a number of people who believed that not only was Waites'
Woman a real supernatural being, but that she still exists today,
waiting to be found.

The following for *The Woman in Time* was initially a group of
misguided but harmless enough amateur historians, enjoying the
'treasure hunt' nature of the book, searching for traces of this
symbolic woman throughout history, occasionally claiming one or
two appearances in sources from the years after Waites' death.

At some point in the mid-seventies – the most conspiracy-
minded of decades before our current one – enthusiasm for the
book seems to have shifted from a handful of treasure hunters
to a smaller group convinced Waites had uncovered a vast
conspiracy to hide an immortal woman within the corridors
of power. Now being on several mailing lists against my will, I
have been informed of a series of newsletters and self-published
books extending Waites' collection of 'sightings' into the
present, with a website and discussion forum currently forming
the meeting place for these fantasists.[1]

This (rather disorganised) organisation claims it aims to
'continue Dorothy Waites' quest to uncover Britain's greatest
secret', and will accept practically any appearance of a woman
of any kind, in any context, as a possible 'sighting'. Throughout
the website's pages we find pictures by the fantasy illustrator

---

1   I am declining to reveal the website's name to avoid
directing more traffic towards it. I will note (without comment)
that after time spent attempting to find those sending me
unpleasant letters, I discovered many of the site's frequent
visitors are also members of groups dedicated to the discussion
of UFO sightings, ghost hunting, and Bigfoot.

Arthur Rackham, statues of The Little Mermaid, depictions of fairies and elves; frankly the vast majority of it belonging firmly within the pages of Tolkien or The Fortean Times.

Whilst Waites peppered her book with references to myths and legends – The Lady of the Lake being listed as one of the mythical iterations of the symbol is referenced here in the play – her interest was in how this <u>symbol</u> had drifted into use within historical record. The contemporary 'Followers of The Woman', as they call themselves,[2] now not only find this symbol in every shadow throughout art and history, but imbue this symbol with an actual life and personality.

Whilst I've been clear that *The Woman in Time* holds no special place in my heart as a serious work of scholarship, it saddens me to see this intelligent (if misguided) woman have her work seized by a group who have wilfully misread it to claim the existence of an immortal woman – to what ends I have no idea.

And if Waites' evidence for her theory was meager, this group have found new, even emptier barrels to scrape:

From the Blitz diary of an ARP Warden for Preston, September 1940
   'Called out bed past twelve last night.
   Mr Cowton in terrible state after claiming to seen a woman up by the cathedral.
   Said he seen her on fire with a hole through the middle.
   All went and had a look what with the times but down to nerves.
   Wouldn't much like to see a thing myself.'

Sheffield Telegraph, 23rd January 1974
   'Local youths have been warned to keep away from the derelict wire works at the edge of town after a fire was reported on Monday evening. No evidence of a fire was

2   Which I find a tad creepy.

found but a young woman was seen fleeing the factory.'

Not even worth commenting on, I'm sure you'll agree.

+

And so here we are, it's 2020, and this is (to my knowledge) the first play about 'The Woman'. Whilst based around the notion of such a woman being real, I am happy to report it is neither dismissive of Waites, nor validates the ludicrous cabal that has sprung up around her. Instead, it roots the idea where it belongs: in fiction.

I should have liked more mention of the book itself, and can't help but feel it might have been best set within an academic institution as a whole, since that is where the real story of the book takes place, but of course I'd think that. I am not a literary critic, nor a dramatic one, and will not be able to see the production itself, so I cannot pass judgement on the play in any artistic sense. But reading through the script I struggle to shake the disappointment that there's not more *history* in the play, especially after the amount of questions Mr McDowell subjected me to.

There are a few changes from Waites' lists of 'distinguishing features', which is to be expected, having transformed 'The Woman' into The Woman; a character with hopes and fears like any other.

In the play she becomes something of a Dickensian, or fairy-tale character; a woman orphaned by time, traipsing up and down the country searching for a home. The central concept of Waites' book has been taken and turned into a picaresque. The Woman despises being turned into 'a story', and is never happier than when living incognito in suburbia.

Interestingly – or frustratingly, depending on your interests – McDowell has sidestepped the specifics of history almost entirely, and instead of drawing the cast of characters from those Waites affiliates with 'The Woman', he has instead surrounded his protagonist with imagined figures from each period, none of which hold positions of any real power.

I found two of these in particular to be of interest:

The Roman soldier who features briefly is in keeping with Waites' book, but feels somewhat lacking. A major part of *The Woman in Time* posits 'The Woman' as a pagan figure kept as a mascot throughout the Roman invasion. Unfortunately, the playwright seems to enjoy stoking the fires of the 'Followers' by setting these appearances in 343AD: the year Western Roman Emperor Constans I made an undocumented trip to England for unknown reasons.

And one can't help but smile at the 'Evan' character, who is every inch the spit of the average Waites fanatic, if better-tempered. I am grateful for the moment – despite the irony – in which he tells us 'The Woman' is a symbol, not a person.

+

The most optimistic of historians believe our path to a utopian future is paved with the knowledge gained by constantly revisiting the past. I'm not sure if I fall quite so firmly in this camp, but I do believe a society that remembers its history fares better than one that chooses to forget it.

This is the one lasting positive I can find from *The Woman in Time*, but I stand by my assertion that living within its pages for too long brings nothing but fantastic notions of immortality, which are useless to our own definitively *mortal* world.

I am pleased Mr McDowell has found a new home for 'The Woman'.

I only hope he's prepared to meet her most ardent fans.

Professor Helen Cullwick lectures in History at The University of Irwell

Methuen Drama Modern Plays

include work by

Bola Agbaje
Edward Albee
Davey Anderson
Jean Anouilh
John Arden
Peter Barnes
Sebastian Barry
Alistair Beaton
Brendan Behan
Edward Bond
William Boyd
Bertolt Brecht
Howard Brenton
Amelia Bullmore
Anthony Burgess
Leo Butler
Jim Cartwright
Lolita Chakrabarti
Caryl Churchill
Lucinda Coxon
Curious Directive
Nick Darke
Shelagh Delaney
Ishy Din
Claire Dowie
David Edgar
David Eldridge
Dario Fo
Michael Frayn
John Godber
Paul Godfrey
James Graham
David Greig
John Guare
Mark Haddon
Peter Handke
David Harrower
Jonathan Harvey
Iain Heggie

Robert Holman
Caroline Horton
Terry Johnson
Sarah Kane
Barrie Keeffe
Doug Lucie
Anders Lustgarten
David Mamet
Patrick Marber
Martin McDonagh
Arthur Miller
D. C. Moore
Tom Murphy
Phyllis Nagy
Anthony Neilson
Peter Nichols
Joe Orton
Joe Penhall
Luigi Pirandello
Stephen Poliakoff
Lucy Prebble
Peter Quilter
Mark Ravenhill
Philip Ridley
Willy Russell
Jean-Paul Sartre
Sam Shepard
Martin Sherman
Wole Soyinka
Simon Stephens
Peter Straughan
Kae Tempest
Theatre Workshop
Judy Upton
Timberlake Wertenbaker
Roy Williams
Snoo Wilson
Frances Ya-Chu Cowhig
Benjamin Zephaniah

For a complete listing of
Methuen Drama titles, visit:
www.bloomsbury.com/drama

Follow us on Twitter and keep up to date
with our news and publications
@MethuenDrama